STORIES IN HISTORY

THE ANCIENT AMERICAS

30,000 B.C.–A.D. 1600

Printed in the United States

ISBN-13: 978-0-618-22210-0
ISBN-10: 0-618-22210-3

  8 9 10 —2266— 15
4500549500

Table of Contents

PART I: EARLY HUNTERS, FARMERS, AND TRADERS

c. 30,000 B.C.
A Search for Early Americans 30
by Judith Conaway

*Lotus helps Dr. Tie-Dye look for evidence of
the earliest humans who lived in the Americas.
Scientists have new ideas about who these
people were and how they lived.*

PART III: MANY NATIONS

About this Book

The stories are historical fiction. They are based on historical fact, but some of the characters and events may be fictional. In the Sources section, you'll learn which is which, and where the information came from.

The illustrations are all historical. If they are from a time different from the story, the caption tells you. Original documents help you understand the time period. Maps let you know where things were.

Items explained in People and Terms to Know are repeated in the Glossary. Look there if you come across a name or term you don't know.

Historians do not always know or agree on the exact dates of events in the past. The letter c before a date means "about" (from the Latin word circa).

If you would like to read more about these exciting times, you will find recommendations in Reading on Your Own.

Background

"The circle of life is never broken."

—Taos Pueblo song

▲

Canyon de Chelly in northern Arizona, home of the Pueblo Indians
and their ancestors.

The First People in America

The First Americans

Thousands of years ago, before the last Ice Age ended, much of North America was covered by ice sheets more than a mile thick. Huge animals roamed through this land, but human beings had not yet arrived.

How did the first humans come to North America? When did they come? How did they live when they got here? To answer these questions, scientists have been searching for clues at ancient settlements. Some answers are beginning to unfold.

For many years, scientists have believed that humans walked to North America from Asia. This might seem impossible because today these two places are separated by the Bering Sea. But during the last Ice Age, sea levels fell. This caused a land bridge (Beringia) to form across the Bering Sea. It connected what is now Siberia, in Asia, to Alaska, in North America. (See map on page 14.)

Bands of Ice Age hunters probably followed the animals they hunted. They followed the woolly mammoth, giant sloth, and mastodon across the land bridge to North America. Over the centuries, the number of these groups increased. Eventually, the hunters reached the east coast of North America and the tip of South America around 9000 or 8000 B.C.

Ice Age Cultures

In the 1930s, near Clovis, New Mexico, scientists found a hunting ground that dated from about 12,000 years ago. Tools, weapons, and other objects were found here. Scientists called the people who made and used these objects the Clovis culture.

Scientists use the word *site* to describe places where they have dug up objects from ancient human life. The Clovis sites were important because scientists believed that the Clovis people were the first to arrive in the Americas. Similar sites, with similar objects, have been found in different places in the Americas. These sites support the idea that all of the different groups of Native Americans can be traced back to the first bands of people who crossed the Bering land bridge.

Most of the Clovis sites that scientists found were not villages, or places where people lived. The sites were places where people killed and butchered the animals they hunted. There weren't many clues about people's everyday lives at these sites.

▲
A scientist examines the bones of a mastodon at a Clovis site in Arizona.

Scientists are still finding new clues about Ice Age peoples. In the 1970s, at Monte Verde in Chile, Dr. Tom Dillehay made an exciting discovery. He found a settlement site. This site seems to be at least 1,000 years older than the Clovis culture. Many scientists agree that it is the earliest human settlement site in the Americas.

The Monte Verde discovery has changed some ideas about the movement of early peoples in the Americas. One idea is that after crossing into the Americas at Beringia, the new arrivals may have

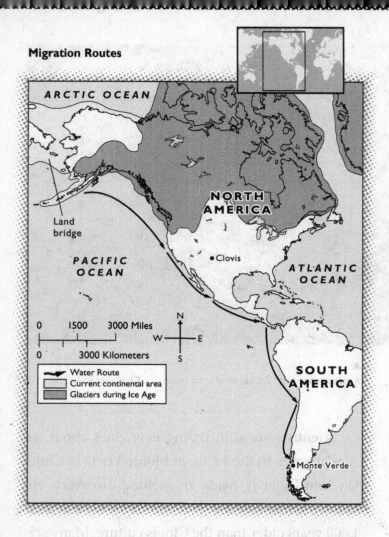

traveled south by boat. Scientists think that humans might have come to the Americas as early as 30,000 years ago—or even earlier.

Some of the objects found at the Monte Verde site help explain how people lived. Dillehay's team found rows of wooden foundations at the Monte Verde site. The foundations held up the frames of shelters. The frames would have been covered with animal skins. Skins stretched over frames made for good shelters. The team also found mastodon meat, trash pits, 70 types of plants, stone tools, parts of wooden canoes, and even a child's footprint.

The Monte Verde site showed that in addition to hunting for food, Ice Age peoples gathered nuts, seeds, berries, and roots. They made tools and weapons from stone, wood, and bone. They traveled by water, as well as over land. And the shelters they built show that Ice Age peoples may have lived in one place for long periods of time.

▲
Stone tools created by Ice Age people were discovered at Monte Verde in Chile.

The End of the Ice Age

The last Ice Age ended around 10,000 B.C. Glaciers melted, sea levels rose, and the land bridge in Beringia was again covered by water.

As North America's climate became warmer, many Ice Age mammals on which early hunters had depended died out. Humans adapted and began hunting smaller animals for food. By 6000 B.C., some groups had moved to the Pacific coast to live on fish and shellfish.

Farming

Simple farming began in Mexico somewhere between 8,000 and 6,000 years ago. Corn was a most important early crop. Farmers later grew squash, peppers, gourds, beans, and cotton. By the first century A.D., corn was being grown in America, in the area where today the borders of New Mexico, Colorado, Utah, and Arizona meet. As time went on, corn became a main crop throughout the Americas.

Early Civilizations

Some of the remarkable early civilizations in the Americas include the Olmec, Maya, Aztec, Inca, Hohokam, Anasazi, and the Mound Builders of the Ohio and Mississippi river valleys.

Olmec

The powerful Olmec culture (about 1200–800 B.C.) developed in the lowland rainforests of what is now eastern Mexico. The Olmecs were skillful farmers, traders, and architects. They used a form of picture writing to record time. They created beautiful pottery, and jewelry. But their most famous creations are huge, flat-faced stone heads that weigh 20 tons each.

Maya

The Mayan culture arose in present-day Guatemala and reached its height from A.D. 300 to 900. At its peak, there were 40 Mayan cities, with populations ranging from 5,000 to 50,000 people.

The Maya built stone pyramids, temples, plazas, and courts for playing ball. They used picture writing and created a 365-day calendar. The Maya were skilled at math and astronomy, and they created exact tables of the positions of the moon and Venus. Mayan farmers used advanced planting and watering methods to grow crops.

The Maya made paper and books, worked gold and copper, and carved beautiful sculpture in stone. They prayed to nature gods in ceremonies that sometimes used human sacrifice.

Aztec

Around A.D. 1200, the Aztec group moved into what is currently central Mexico. There they helped to bring down the Toltecs, the largest, most important tribe of that region. The Aztecs later

◀ A page from an Aztec book, the Codex Mendoza, shows the founding of Tenochtitlán, the capital city of the Aztecs.

founded Tenochtitlán, their capital, on the site of today's Mexico City.

By the time of Emperor Montezuma II (1502–1520), the Aztecs controlled most of Mexico. The powerful emperor ruled many millions of people—some say as many as 12 million. The communities throughout the empire had local governors and courts. They all reported back to the government in the capital city of Tenochtitlán.

The Aztecs prayed to nature gods. They developed improved farming methods. And their knowledge of building, math, and astronomy was great. Tenochtitlán, like all great capital cities, had beautiful palaces, gardens, a library, and a huge, busy market.

When the Spanish arrived in Tenochtitlán in 1519, they were amazed by the wealth of the Aztecs. In 1521, Spaniard Hernán Cortés captured and destroyed Tenochtitlán. He then built Mexico City in its place.

Inca

A few years later, another Spanish conqueror, Francisco Pizarro, arrived in Peru with 180 men. There the Inca controlled an empire of 12 million people that stretched more than 2,000 miles along South America's Pacific coast. The Inca had built two north–south roads, each 2,250 miles long, to help unite their empire.

The Inca, too, prayed to nature gods. Sometimes they practiced animal and human sacrifice. Most Incas were farmers. They lived in houses of stone or adobe (sun-dried bricks) and raised llamas, dogs, alpaca, and guinea pigs. They used advanced farming methods to grow corn, squash, potatoes, and other crops. Their mountain cities such as Cuzco and Machu Picchu had stone buildings, temples, and strong fortresses.

Even though the Incas outnumbered the Spanish explorers, the Spanish conqueror Pizarro had the advantage of European weapons. After capturing and murdering the Incan emperor, Pizarro conquered the empire.

Mound Builders

East of the Mississippi River, ancient peoples called Mound Builders emerged between about 400 B.C. and A.D. 1700. The Adena, Hopewell, and Mississippian cultures developed one after another. They are called "Mound Builders" because they built many large earth mounds. The famous Serpent Mound in Ohio is nearly a quarter of a mile long and averages three feet high.

The Adena culture was mostly in what is now southern Ohio. The Adena used poles, bark, and willows to build villages of circular houses. They buried their dead in large mounds that they built with packed earth. The Adena lived by hunting, gathering, fishing, and raising corn.

Several centuries later, the Hopewell people built villages along rivers and streams in the same region as the Adena. The Hopewell were also hunters, gatherers, and farmers. They created beautiful pottery and metalwork and traded with different people throughout North America. Shells from the Mississippi and the Gulf Coast, copper from the Great Lakes region, and grizzly bear teeth from the Rockies have all been found in Hopewell mounds.

The Mississippian people, the last group of Mound

This pipe was created by the Adena Indians, who lived in Ohio during the 8th and 9th centuries A.D. It was found in 1901 in a huge burial mound near Chillicothe, Ohio.

Builders, were farmers. Their city of Cahokia, near modern-day St. Louis, Missouri, had hundreds of mounds, including the largest mound in North America. By A.D. 1200, as many as 10,000 people lived at Cahokia. Some of its mounds can still be seen today.

Hohokam and Anasazi

In North America's southwestern desert areas, ancient Native American peoples such as the Hohokam and Anasazi grew corn, squash, and beans.

The Hohokam lived in what is now central and southern Arizona from about 300 B.C. to A.D. 1400. They are most famous for their 150-mile network of canals, which watered their fields and helped them to grow corn and cotton. The Hohokam built adobe houses around town squares.

From around A.D. 100, the Anasazi developed an important civilization. They lived in the area where the boundaries of Arizona, New Mexico, Colorado, and Utah now meet. Anasazi houses changed over the years from simple tentlike structures to large stone houses to cliff dwellings that sometimes rose four stories high and had as many as 1,000 rooms. The Anasazi were mainly farmers who grew pumpkins, beans, and corn.

Native Americans in 1600

When Europeans began to arrive in the 1500s, there were about 240 different Native American cultures living in North America. Their customs and

▲
A Hopi priest photographed in 1910 is dressed for the sacred Snake Dance, which had been celebrated by his people for hundreds of years.

ways of life varied because different groups had adapted to the regions in which they lived.

North and Northwest Coast

Native Americans in the north and northwest regions enjoyed the riches of the rivers and the sea. They fished for salmon, gathered shellfish, and hunted for sea mammals and birds. They built canoes and dwellings out of wood from the forests. They made clothing and blankets from bark fibers and mountain-goat wool. Their villages were governed by groups of tribal elders.

West

In the West, Shoshone-speaking Native Americans moved from place to place in family groups, searching for the wild seeds, insects, and small mammals that were their food. Sometimes families joined together for hunting or special celebrations. Around 1700, after horses were brought to North America, they became mounted hunters and warriors.

Southwest

By 1500, farming groups like the Pueblo had lived for centuries in the Southwest. The Pueblo were skilled at crafts. They built special adobe houses

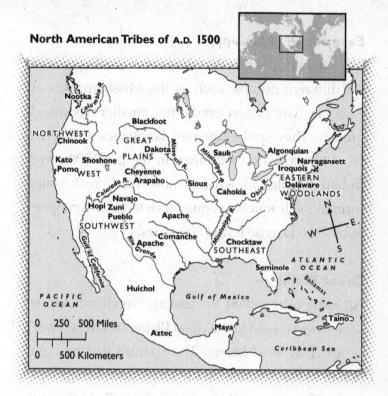

North American Tribes of A.D. 1500

Nootka
Columbia R.
NORTHWEST
Chinook
Kato Shoshone
Pomo WEST
Colorado R.
Navajo
Hopi Zuni
Pueblo
SOUTHWEST
Apache
Rio Grande
Blackfoot
GREAT
PLAINS
Dakota
Cheyenne
Arapaho
Sioux
Comanche
Apache
Missouri R.
Mississippi R.
Sauk
Cahokia
Ohio R.
Mississippi R.
Chocktaw
SOUTHEAST
Algonquian
Iroquois
Narragansett
EASTERN
Delaware
WOODLANDS
Seminole

PACIFIC
OCEAN

Huichol

Gulf of California

Gulf of Mexico

ATLANTIC
OCEAN

Bahamas

Taino

0   250 500 Miles

0   500 Kilometers

Aztec   Maya

Caribbean Sea

N
W E
S

that had many apartments. The Navajo and Apache also lived in the Southwest. The Navajo, who probably moved from Canada around A.D. 1000, were influenced by Pueblo arts, architecture, and weaving. The Apache remained hunters and gatherers.

East of the Mississippi

The Mississippi and Ohio rivers were trading routes for different groups, such as the Mississippians at Cahokia. Farther east lived other, smaller woodland groups. They spoke different languages and often went to war with each other. In the late 1500s, five Indian peoples in what is now New York state, formed the Iroquois League for defense and cooperation. The League lasted 200 years.

Great Plains

As Europeans settled the eastern woodlands, some tribes moved west to the Great Plains area, where few people had lived before. The Spanish had brought horses to the Americas in the 1500s, and such groups as the Cheyenne and Sioux became skilled at riding them. With horses they developed a new way of life built around buffalo hunts and warfare.

Southeast

In the Southeast, Native American tribes such as the Creek and Choctaw built towns with town squares and public and religious buildings. These tribes lived by hunting, by gathering fruits and nuts, and by growing crops such as corn, pumpkins, beans, and tobacco.

Changing Cultures

The story of the early Americans is a story of changing cultures. By the 1500s, some cultures, such as the Aztecs, had developed complex civilizations. Others, such as the Taino, who were the first Native Americans that Christopher Columbus met, had developed very simple cultures.

Native Americans had survived for thousands of years by adapting to changing conditions. But nothing had prepared them for contact with Europeans. Some thought the strange looking, pale Europeans were gods. Some thought the Europeans were just travelers. The Native Americans all wanted to trade food and other goods for the Europeans' strong metal tools and weapons.

Native American stone weapons were no match for European guns and swords. And Europeans brought something to the Americas that was even more deadly to Native Americans than guns—disease.

The Native Americans had no time to adapt to the diseases brought by European explorers and settlers. Disease and lack of good weapons gave Native Americans little chance to hold off European conquest.

Time Line

c. 30,000 B.C.—People begin to cross the Beringia land bridge.

10,000 B.C.—Land bridge disappears, ending migrations. Clovis culture begins.

6000 B.C.—Corn is farmed.

1200 B.C.—Olmec culture begins.

400 B.C.—Hopewell culture begins.

300 B.C.—Hohokam culture begins.

A.D. 300–900—Mayan culture is at its height.

800—Mississippian culture begins.

1000—Vikings reach Newfoundland.

1050–1300—Anasazi build cliff dwellings.

1100–1200—Cahokia is at its peak.

1200s—Aztecs invade present-day Mexico.

1325—Aztecs found Tenochtitlán.

1400s—The Inca establish their empire.

1492—Columbus reaches the Americas.

c. 1570—League of the Iroquois founded.

1519–1521—Aztecs conquered by Spanish.

PART TWO

Early Hunters, Farmers, and Traders

A Search for Early Americans

BY JUDITH CONAWAY

"**P**lease pass the goop," said Lotus.

Dr. "Tie-Dye" handed Lotus a clay jar. "Here's a new jar. I mixed it up myself, just yesterday."

Lotus took the jar with thanks. There was no doubt about it. Dr. Tie knew her stuff. The goop was made from plants. It really did the job when it came to **coiling** twine. It kept your skin from being torn up by the plant fibers, and it helped hold the fibers together.

Lotus was spending the summer working on an **archaeology** dig. It was nothing like what she'd

---

People and Terms to Know

coiling—way of making rope or twine from plant fibers by twisting multiple strands of the fibers around each other.

archaeology (AHR•kee•AHL•uh•jee)—study of ancient civilizations. Scientists who study archaeology are known as archaeologists.

Found at Monte Verde, this twisted reed twine held stones that could be

expected. For one thing, she hardly ever got to work on the **excavation** itself. Instead, she and the other students were helping Dr. Tie explore the nearby area.

It wasn't very exciting. But Dr. Tie was cool. She joked around with them a lot. And she didn't mind that they called her Dr. Tie-Dye. (She owned the largest collection of tie-dyed T-shirts any of them had ever seen.)

D r. Tie was a scientist who studied ancient seeds and other plant matter. She tried to discover whether humans had ever used the plants. She would begin by looking for similar plants that still grow wild. Then she would find out if the local people used these plants. She would take her students to meet local people and learn their skills.

That's why Lotus was now sitting on the ground with her left leg tucked under her stretched-out right leg, coiling twine.

Lotus smeared the goop over her right knee. She draped the twine over her knee and rolled it with

---

People and Terms to Know

excavation (EX•kuh•VAY•shuhn)—process of digging out or uncovering ancient ruins; an archaeological site or dig.

her right palm. She took two strips of plant fiber from the pile and put the ends into the twine. She rolled some more, always in the same direction. She reached for two more strips of fiber.

In no time, she was coiling twine quickly and tightly. She stopped every few minutes to wind the newly coiled twine around its stick and smear more goop on her leg.

Dr. Tie had gone back to work, over on the opposite bank of the creek. Lotus hoped Dr. Tie would find what she was looking for—signs of places where people lived, hunted, fished, or explored. **Carbon dating** showed the layer she was digging to be about 15,000 years old. In that layer, Dr. Tie had found evidence of many plants used by humans. But it wasn't enough.

"We need artifacts to prove there were people here."

"We need **artifacts** to prove there were people here," she was always reminding her students. "Human bones would be even better. The next best

People and Terms to Know

carbon dating—method of finding the age of an object by measuring two types of carbon atoms it contains. Because the ratio of these two atoms changes after a living thing dies, scientists can use the measurement to figure out how long ago the living materials in it died.

artifacts—human-made objects remaining from early civilizations. Even broken pieces of artifacts interest archaeologists.

find would be something that people made or that was clearly put there by people."

Dr. Tie was one of many scientists with new ideas about the first people of the Americas. The new ideas were causing big arguments among archaeologists. Lotus and the other students had been hearing the arguments for weeks, as they worked on the dig. While Lotus coiled the twine, her mind wandered back over what she had learned.

The archaeologists agreed that people probably entered the Americas through Asia, by way of what is now Alaska. But they disagreed about how long ago people arrived in the Americas, how they traveled, what route they took, and how they lived.

Most archaeologists thought the first people arrived during the last **Ice Age**. At that time, sea levels were low. A land bridge formed across the Bering Sea. Herds of large animals moved across this land bridge. Hunters followed the animals. Objects found at archaeological **sites** seemed to support this idea.

People and Terms to Know

Ice Age—part of geological time when the earth's temperature was colder, causing large parts of the planet to be covered in glaciers (huge masses of ice). It ended about 10,000 years ago.

sites—places; archaeological sites are places where scientists dig up objects from ancient human life.

The most important sites were those of the **Clovis culture**. At Clovis sites, archaeologists found thousands of spear points, clearly made by human hands. These artifacts were often found with the bones of **mammoths**, **bison**, camels, and other large animals.

The oldest known Clovis sites were dated to about 12,000 years ago. So archaeologists thought that humans could not have reached the Americas until about 12,500 years ago, or 10,500 B.C. Most scientists accepted this date. Lotus remembered reading it in her history textbooks.

Now many archaeologists were saying that Clovis people were not the first. Material found at a site called **Monte Verde** had been dated to 13,700 years ago.

People and Terms to Know

Clovis culture—way of life that was followed by ancient people who hunted large animals using spears. The culture is named for Clovis, New Mexico, the first site in the Americas where human weapons were found along with the bones of Ice Age animals.

mammoths—large elephant-like animals that once lived in North America. They became extinct in prehistoric times.

bison (BY•suhn)—large hoofed mammal having a dark brown coat, shaggy mane, and short, curved horns; also known as buffalo.

Monte Verde—archaeological site located near the coast of southern Chile. Dr. Tom Dillehay and other archaeologists from the United States and Chile began excavating the site in 1977. Their discoveries were not officially dated and accepted until 1997.

Monte Verde was an ancient campsite that flooded and was then buried in **peat**. The peat preserved hundreds of artifacts, including digging sticks, spears, stone cutting tools, and wooden stakes tied with twine. There were remains of at least twelve houses, which seem to have been wooden frames covered with animal skins. Most exciting of all, there was a tiny human footprint, probably made by a child.

Some scientists now thought that people came to the Americas at least 30,000 years ago.

Monte Verde and other sites showed that people had been adapting to their environment for quite a long time. Some scientists now thought that people came to the Americas at least 30,000 years ago.

How could people have traveled so long ago, when much of North America was buried under ice? Archaeologists point out that during the last Ice

People and Terms to Know

peat—partly decayed form of plant matter that is found in swamps and bogs. Peat provides a wet, oxygen-free environment, protecting materials from bacteria and decay.

An archaeologist brushes away dirt to reveal an artifact at an excavation site.

Age the sea levels were lower than they are now. It would have been possible for people to travel along the coastline in boats.

The movement to Monte Verde probably took place over a long period of time. People would stay in one place as long as there was enough food. When they had to move, they would send explorers ahead. Once explorers had found a new place, their families would follow.

Scientific ideas about ancient diets were changing as well. The remains found at Monte Verde showed that prehistoric people ate plant leaves, seeds, nuts, fruits, fish and other seafood, and small animals.

"These new discoveries put women, children, and old people back into the ancient picture," Dr. Tie had explained to Lotus and the others. "The old idea of muscular young men hunting big game with spears is no longer right. Now we have a completely different picture of everyday life in ancient times."

Lotus stood up, stretched, and took a drink from her canteen. The afternoon was starting to cool off. She was stiff from sitting.

"Lotus!" called Dr. Tie suddenly. She sounded excited. "Lotus! Bring your twine over here, right away, please!"

Lotus obeyed. The other students followed. The archaeologists nearby left their work. Soon they were all peering over Dr. Tie's shoulder. There it was, caught in the 13,000-year-old layer. They had found a piece of coiled twine.

Wild cheering broke out. Lotus couldn't stop grinning. She had coiled the twine that made the identification! She hugged all the other students and archaeologists, even the ones she didn't know. She got her picture taken with the artifact *in situ*.

"You did it!" she said as she hugged Dr. Tie-Dye. "You found your artifact! How does it feel?"

"Great!" replied Dr. Tie. "Except for my hands. They're almost raw from the digging and from all the handshaking. Would you mind sharing some of that goop?"

QUESTIONS TO CONSIDER

1. According to the generally accepted scientific view, when and how did the earliest Native Americans reach the Western Hemisphere?

2. What effect did the discoveries at Monte Verde have on this view?

3. What did you learn from this story about how the ancient people at Monte Verde lived?

4. What did Dr. Tie mean when she said their discoveries "put women, children, and old people back into the ancient picture"?

People and Terms to Know

in situ (ihn SY•too)—Latin for "in place." Archaeologists document their discoveries exactly as they are found. No one can move artifacts until they have been measured and photographed *in situ*. This helps the archaeologists to date the artifacts and to prove the layers have not been disturbed.

Clovis Hunters Kill a Mammoth

BY WALTER HAZEN

$\mathbf{M}$arshall McIntyre sat at his desk, yawning. Unknown to his parents, he had stayed up late the night before watching television in his room. He was very sleepy and was struggling to stay awake. Mrs. Wilson's voice was becoming less and less clear.

"Now, class," she had said, "today we're going to study the Clovis People of North America. We're going to learn how they pursued the woolly mammoth and became some of the first big game hunters."

Big woof, Marshall thought. *Who cares?*

Mrs. Wilson continued to talk about the early North American Indians. She was describing how they lived at the end of the last Ice Age.

Spears in hand, Clovis hunters sneak up on a woolly mammoth. Working together, they could bring down a mammoth big enough to feed the whole group for weeks.

Yeah, thought Marshall, *way back when it was cold most of the time and people had to strike a couple of rocks together just to make a fire. Everybody ran around in clothes made of animal skins and lived either in caves or shelters made of hide.*

Mrs. Wilson started talking about the woolly mammoth. It was some kind of ancient elephant.

What a beast! Marshall shuddered. It had two large, curved tusks and was covered all over with hair. It stood from 11 to 13 feet high at the shoulder.

Think about that! Thirteen feet! That's two of High-rise Higgins, our star basketball player.

Marshall's head nodded in sleep. In a flash he was transported back 12,000 years to some place in what is now Canada.

This is strange; I feel I belong here. I'm not some twenty-first-century kid with a computer and a room full of CDs. I'm a Clovis kid.

He looked down at his shirt. It was hairy.

I've got on a bison robe! And this isn't a pencil in my hand, it's a spear!

He looked around.

Dad's here too. And he's not in his usual business suit. He's also wearing a bison robe. Where's Mom? She's probably in some cave scraping an animal hide or something.

"Son, are you ready?"

"Ready, Dad," Marshall answered.

Dad told him to follow. Marshall stood up and went with him. Marshall felt excited and frightened at the same time. He had a lump the size of a **saber-toothed tiger** in his throat. He was 12 years old; it was time to get on with this business of becoming a man.

Marshall felt excited and frightened at the same time.

They set out. There were ten of them. The Clovis lived in small groups of about twenty people. If they killed just one mammoth, it would give them enough food for a long time. (Sometimes they would join with other **clans** for a hunt. They would charge at the mammoths and drive them off a high cliff. Then they would use spears to finish off the animals that were not killed by the fall. But this was not one of those times.)

People and Terms to Know

saber-toothed tiger—large Ice Age cat with two very long upper teeth.
clans—large groups of families that claim a common ancestor.

Marshall looked at his spear. *This is not your ordinary, ancient spear. No sir! We must be far too advanced for that.* The spear point was fluted. Someone had chipped a groove down the entire length of the point then split the wooden spear at the end. Each side of the spear was fitted into the point's two grooves. Then the point had been tied to the spear with a piece of leather. *This is a pretty nifty weapon.*

If he had tried, Marshall would have discovered that he couldn't throw the spear with enough force to pierce the tough hide of a mammoth. Even the strongest man in their group couldn't do that. Dad handed him a throwing thing archaeologists would later call an **atlatl**. It was made of wood and was about the length of Dad's arm. At one end of the atlatl was a cup. Marshall watched Dad set the end of the spear in the cup. With a quick flip of his arm and wrist, he sent the spear hurling with tremendous force.

People and Terms to Know

atlatl (aht•LAHT•l)—spear-throwing device usually made of a stick with a thong or socket to hold the spear steady. It added force to the spear-thrower's thrust.

Native American with a spear and an atlatl.

Marshall tried it. What a joke. The spear wobbled in the cup. Before Marshall had his arm halfway back, the spear toppled out. He tried again. Worse, just as he was about to hurl it, the spear fell out and barely missed his foot. He looked around quickly. He hoped no one had seen what he'd just done. Spear-throwing was a lot harder than it looked. The others had probably been practicing from the time they were four years old!

Dad didn't seem to notice. He waved him on to join the others. A short time later, one of the men in the lead spotted a mammoth. Marshall gasped. It was huge! He really hadn't expected that it would be so big. There it was, shaking the ground each time it took a step. Its feet looked as if they could crush large rocks, and its giant tusks looked as if they were made to stick in a twelve-year-old boy. The animal terrified him!

There it was, shaking the ground each time it took a step.

Everyone stood very still. Men fitted their spears into their atlatls. Marshall held his spear so it didn't tumble out of the cup. He didn't so much as breathe.

Dad gave the signal to attack. Nine arms drew back to hurl the deadly spears. Marshall couldn't hurl his. He just stood there. Nine spears broke through the tough hide. One must have pierced the mammoth's heart, because it reeled and rocked and finally fell over and went still.

The men shouted and clapped and cheered. (No one noticed as Marshall quickly kicked his spear into a tangle of grasses.) They had been running short of food, but now they would have enough to last for a good while. The mammoth would give them more than just food. Its hide would be used for clothing and for thongs to tie things down. Tusks and bones would be used to make weapons and tools. Rib bones would become supports over which hides would be stretched to provide shelters. Even the mammoth's brains were used—for **tanning** the hide. No part of the beast was wasted.

They walked back to camp, laughing and slapping each other in rough-and-tumble joy. But, Marshall wondered, was he now a man?

The laughter became louder. It was aimed at him. But it wasn't coming from the Clovis hunters. He looked up in time to see an amused look on Mrs. Wilson's face turn serious again.

QUESTIONS TO CONSIDER

1. What is a mammoth and why was it important to the Clovis people?
2. What is an atlatl and how does it work?
3. Why do you think Marshall couldn't throw a spear with his atlatl?

People and Terms to Know

tanning—process of making leather from rawhides.

Carvers of the Mound Builders

BY BARBARA LITTMAN

Carving was what the men in Diving Turtle's family did. And to become a carver was Diving Turtle's greatest dream. His father, Smoke Shaper, was one of the village's most respected carvers. He had left on a trading mission many months ago. Since then, Running Bear, the boy's grandfather, had grown weaker and weaker. Now, the boy longed for his father's return.

"Maybe today is the day Smoke Shaper will come home," he thought as he climbed the **rampart** along the river bank. Smoke Shaper and the other traders had headed east, then north,

---

People and Terms to Know

rampart—wide, raised mound of earth—built for protection from flooding.

The tobacco bowl on this pipe is shaped like a beaver. It was carved from
stone and decorated with bone and pearl by a carver who lived near
Hopewell, Ohio, about A.D. 300.

hoping to return with a good supply of **mica** for mirrors and **pipestone** for carving. So much had happened since they left. "Now the mica might be needed to line my grandfather's tomb," thought Diving Turtle.

Diving Turtle dumped a basket of trash from his wigwam's fall harvesting. Then he sat quietly on the rampart. He looked across the **flood plain** and then upstream. He tried to see even a small movement that might mean people were coming. Hard as he looked though, he could see no one coming.

"Father must return soon, before Running Bear moves on to the spirit world," thought Diving Turtle as he reached inside his pouch. Yes, it was still there: his first pipe carved from pipestone. Diving Turtle had watched his father closely as he chipped and smoothed pipestone. Often while his father was carving, he would tell Diving Turtle

---

People and Terms to Know

mica (MY•kuh)—shiny rock that can be split into large sheets. The Mound Builders got it from the area of present-day North Carolina.

pipestone—soft, red stone found in Minnesota, the Dakotas, and in Canada. The Mound Builders used it for carving.

flood plain—flat land that borders a river and is made of soil deposited during floods.

about the mountains far to the north where they got the pipestone. Diving Turtle prayed that his first carving would convince his father he was worthy of the title "carver."

Diving Turtle prayed that his first carving would convince his father he was worthy of the title "carver."

Several dogs, looking for food, sniffed around Diving Turtle. Giving one a pat, he picked up his empty basket and turned back to the village. It was still early, but many people were already hard at work. His sister and two friends were going out to the fields to gather wild sump weed and goosewood seeds. He had heard his mother saying last night that they should keep the largest seeds separate from the rest. The smaller seeds could be used for flour and the larger seeds for planting in the spring.

Diving Turtle's friend, Black Hawk, had already restarted the smoking fire. Several women were spreading ducks and fish across the poles to smoke and dry the flesh for winter. Diving Turtle's mouth watered as he thought of the stew his mother made from dried duck and ground nuts.

H is aunt and three other women were weaving nearby. Their copper earrings and pearl necklaces swayed with the regular movement of their hands over the looms. At this time of year, the mats they wove were simple. But this year, a special one was being made from thick milkweed. Bits of fur and yarn were being added for color. This was an important mat. It would be his grandfather's burial **shroud**.

Diving Turtle's mother and sister-in-law had been feeding his grandfather willow-bark tea for a week. Willow-bark tea was a strong medicine. Yet it did not seem strong enough for Running Bear. He was old and weak with fever. Last night, the medicine man had placed the masks around his bed. Their bright red wooden faces were scary. Sometimes they were strong enough to drive away the forest spirits that made men sick. Diving Turtle hoped they would be strong enough this time.

Three days ago though, everyone had agreed: it was time to begin preparing a new **burial mound**. A carver and leader as great and wise as Running Bear must be properly cared for when he left for

---

People and Terms to Know

shroud—cloth used to wrap a body for burial.
burial mound—mound of earth in which the dead were buried.

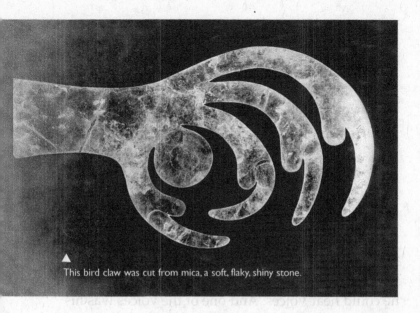
This bird claw was cut from mica, a soft, flaky, shiny stone.

the spirit world. Men and women were carrying baskets of earth up the burial mound and dumping them near the stakes that showed the location of the new tomb.

Diving Turtle knew that treasures were being collected for his grandfather's burial. Copper breastplates and earplugs, long necklaces of pearls and carved conch shells, and pipes carved with rich details were already piled high.

Many of the village's best carvers were working on special pipes to show their respect for his grandfather. The bear and turtle pipes would be some of the finest in the village when the carvers were finished.

If only his father would return. The hot days of summer had already given way to the crisp mornings of early autumn. Smoke Shaper and the rest of the group would have to spend the winter with another tribe if they didn't return soon. "Maybe he'll come home tomorrow," thought Diving Turtle.

The next morning was one of the coldest yet. Diving Turtle could see his breath as he climbed the rampart to dump his wigwam's trash basket. He could see nothing on the river through the mist. But he could hear voices. And one of the voices was his father's! He was sure of it. He never knew if they would return on land or by river. This time it was by river. Diving Turtle ran toward the voices and began to shout. "Father, Father! Here! Bring your canoes in here."

Diving Turtle heard a happy shout in return. Then he saw three canoes coming through the mist. The next thing he knew, he was helping to pull the canoes up onto the rampart. They were loaded with sheets of mica and chunks of pipestone. It had been a good trip.

The dogs were barking and prancing around the group as they came over the top. It didn't take long for the villagers to hear the dogs and know what was happening. Men, women, and children were soon running up the rampart. Everyone was laughing or hugging someone. Diving Turtle's mother stood quietly to the side, as was her way. She waited until Smoke Shaper turned in her direction. Then they were hugging and exchanging news as they went down the rampart.

Smoke Shaper would begin to carve a special pipe to go with his father to the spirit world.

Diving Turtle knew from his father's face that his mother had told him about Running Bear. He watched as Smoke Shaper pulled aside the flap on the wigwam where his father was being cared for. Diving Turtle would never know what they said. He did know, though, that Smoke Shaper would listen carefully to Running Bear. Then, Smoke Shaper would begin to carve a special pipe to go with his father to the spirit world.

* * *

Diving Turtle stood over his father as he chipped and smoothed the pipestone. He could see a large bear, almost a foot long, beginning to take shape. He reached inside his pouch and took a deep breath.

"Father," he said, "I have missed you and thought every day of your hands carving beautiful pipes. I have made a gift to celebrate your return."

He pulled his closed fist from his pouch and opened it in front of his father's eyes. He watched his father closely. He saw no smile, heard no sound. Diving Turtle was afraid. Maybe his pipe was poorly made. Maybe his father was insulted.

Then, he saw the telltale wrinkles around his father's eyes that meant a smile was coming.

"You carved this, my son?" he said, looking hard into his eyes.

"Yes, father. I made it as a gift for you."

"Then may I have it now?" he said, touching the pipe in Diving Turtle's hand.

As Diving Turtle handed the pipe to his father, Smoke Shaper got to his feet and said, "Come with me."

Now Diving Turtle was confused. Maybe the pipe didn't please his father after all. His heart pounding and his feet dragging, he followed his father.

"But why are we going here?" he asked as his father pulled aside the flap where Running Bear's burial gifts were piled. Diving Turtle's breath caught in his throat when he looked at the pile now. It was twice as large as it had been. Beautifully carved antlers and pieces of **obsidian**, pottery bowls, and hand-shaped mica mirrors had been added to the pipes, necklaces, and copper jewelry.

Smoke Shaper turned to Diving Turtle and handed him his little gift pipe.

Smoke Shaper turned to Diving Turtle and handed him his little gift pipe. He nodded at the pile, and then smiled at his son. "Running Bear will need this pipe in the spirit world," he said. "The first pipe carved by the next village carver will smooth his journey. Will you add it to the burial gifts?"

At first Diving Turtle did not understand. His father smiled and nodded again. Then Diving Turtle understood. His pipe was well-carved. His father was pleased. His grandfather would have the best gift he could ever give him.

People and Terms to Know

obsidian (uhb•SIHD•ee•uhn)—shiny, black glass of volcanic origin.

Then, Diving Turtle, son of the son of one of the village's most respected carvers, would be a carver too.

* * *

Carving was one of many crafts which Diving Turtle's people practiced. Diving Turtle's people lived 1,800 years ago in the river valley near present-day Hopewell, Ohio. They had large trading networks across the continent. (See the map on page 59.) Through these networks, they got the metals and other materials they needed to make everyday objects, jewelry, and religious objects. Such objects were buried with their dead in the earthen mounds in each village. Today, because of these burial mounds, Diving Turtle's people are known as **Mound Builders**.

People and Terms to Know

Mound Builders—group of early North American people who developed a way of life in the Ohio and Mississippi valleys from around 500–400 B.C. to 1500 A.D.

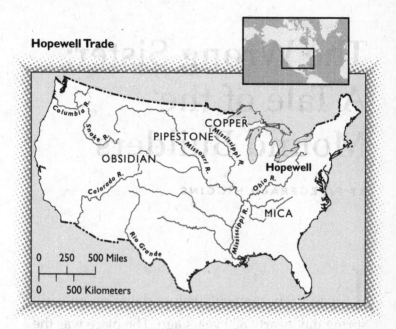

Hopewell Trade

COPPER
PIPESTONE
OBSIDIAN
Columbia R.
Snake R.
Missouri R.
Mississippi R.
Colorado R.
Rio Grande
Ohio R.
Hopewell
MICA
Mississippi R.

0   250   500 Miles

0   500 Kilometers

QUESTIONS TO CONSIDER

1. What kinds of food did the Mound Builders eat? How did they get their food and how did they prepare it?

2. How did the Mound Builders treat illness?

3. Why did the people prepare such elaborate burial mounds?

4. What kinds of skills did the Mound Builders seem to value?

The Wrong Sister: A Tale of the Mound Builders

BY FITZGERALD HIGGINS

It was a few moments before dawn on an early spring day nearly 800 years ago. The place was the city of **Cahokia** near the Mississippi River. A young girl of about fifteen stood in the doorway of her family's home. Her name was Sparrow. She was dressed in a skirt of soft, worn deerskin. Sparrow's round, brown face was not very pretty. But people were attracted to her because usually her face was bright and good-humored. Recently, however, Sparrow had been crying. In one hand, she held a ragged doll made out of cornstalks that had been given to her when she was a child.

People and Terms to Know

Cahokia (kuh•HOH•kee•uh)—name given by archaeologists to an ancient American Indian city in southwestern Illinois.

A modern artist shows the city of Cahokia as it may have looked in A.D. 1150.

Cahokia was the center of a rich land. The flooding of the river made the soil very **fertile**, so the people who lived there were able to grow great crops of corn, beans, pumpkins, squash, and sunflowers. In the nearby forests they gathered huge harvests of fruits, berries, and nuts. The woods and waters were full of birds, beasts, and fish.

The people here belonged to one of the American Indian groups known as Mound Builders. Centuries before, their **ancestors** had built a city. Now thousands of people lived in the city and in the dozens of villages around it.

The city had many high mounds made out of hard-packed earth. On the tops of these mounds were the temples of the people's gods and the homes of their great chief, the priests, and the leaders. In the city below, there were houses, streets, town squares, playing fields, warehouses, and docks. The central part of the city was enclosed

---

People and Terms to Know

fertile (FUR•tl)—able to produce crops.
ancestors (AN•sehs•tuhrz)—people from whom one is descended; early members of one's family; forerunners.

within a high **stockade** of huge tree trunks that was more than two miles around.

Most of the people lived in homes built of **saplings** covered with mats made from the cattails and reeds that grew in the nearby streams. The houses had steeply pitched roofs made from the tall grasses of the surrounding **prairies**.

She stared at the great mound that was the center of her city.

Sparrow looked out across the wide town square where the men and boys played games. She stared at the great mound that was the center of her city. On top of this mound, which was 100 feet high, was the home of their great chief. The sun was rising behind the mound. Sparrow sniffed, then sighed deeply, and finally held up her doll so that it could see the dawn.

"Look, little sister, see the sun rising behind the house of his brother, our chief. That means spring is finally here. It's time to plant our crops. Soon the markets will reopen here. All the different traders and craft makers will come again. We'll see the

People and Terms to Know

stockade (stah•KAYD)—defensive barrier made of strong posts or timbers driven upright side by side into the ground.

saplings (SAP•lihngz)—young trees.

prairies—wide, level areas of flat or rolling grassland, especially the large plain of central North America.

food-sellers and those who gather healing plants. The basket weavers like our family will bring their goods. So will those who shape pots or weave mats or chip flint for tools. Traders will come down the great river from the northern lakes with bright copper. And"—she sighed deeply again—"fine, strong, young men will make the long, hard journey up the river with shells and sharks' teeth from the southern sea.

"Remember last spring when the market opened? One of the shell traders came to our booth looking for baskets for his goods. Our older sister, Willow, was tending the booth with me that day. I must say, she is lovely, with her beautiful face and tall, graceful figure. And unlike you and me, she does know how to dress." Here, she sadly compared her doll's worn cornstalk "dress" and her own shabby deerskin skirt.

"However," she said, "between you and me, Willow is also silly and selfish. But the men never notice that. They just fall in love with her! Remember the young shell trader from the south? He was no different. As soon as he saw her, he was lost. She, of course, hardly noticed him. Willow never pays attention to any man unless he is richly dressed and followed by a lot of servants. But I noticed him. His face had a wonderful strength and sweetness. It was also—until he met my sister—a happy face. But she changed that.

Our great chief is brother to the sun in the sky.

"For many days, he stayed around our booth, trying to win Willow over. He made gifts to her of his most beautiful shells, but it was no use. No simple trader stands a chance with her. She intends to marry a wealthy man and live in a fine house. I told him that, but of course he didn't listen.

"He and I spent a lot of time together during those days. I tried to get his mind off my sister by telling him about the wonders of the city. I told him that our great chief is brother to the sun in the sky. I pointed out that the chief, the priests, and the clan leaders live in splendor on the tops of the high mounds. I told him about the poor workers who dig endless loads of earth from pits and carry them in baskets on their backs to build the mounds. I told him how our wise men use the shadows cast by a circle of posts driven into the ground to follow the passing of the seasons.

"I told him about the chunkey games in the town square. He was only half listening when I described how one of the two players rolls a stone disk swiftly

▲

The circle of posts that the people of Cahokia used to measure time and the passing seasons.

down a path. Then both players race after the disk, each throwing a spear as close as they can to the point where the disk will stop. The player whose spear is closest wins. He seemed more interested when I told him about the gamblers who bet everything they owned on the skill of the chunkey players.

"When the young shell trader's gifts didn't work with Willow, he grew desperate. He took the remainder of his shells over to the central area of the great plaza where the young men played chunkey. He joined the gamblers who stood around and bet on the results. At first, he won. He brought the bearskins and copper pieces and the rest of his winnings over to our house and offered them to Willow if she would be his wife. She still rejected him. He gambled more, hoping to become rich enough to attract her. In the end, of course, he lost everything.

"I comforted him as best I could. He gathered the few things he had left and prepared to return down the great river. I gave him food for his long trip home. When his canoe was going around the bend of the river and I was sure he wouldn't be able to hear me, I shouted, 'You fool! Why did you have to pick the wrong sister?'"

◀ Stone sculpture found at Cahokia shows a mother holding her baby.

Sparrow stopped speaking to her doll and stood quietly looking down at the ground. That's why she didn't notice the figure that came from the shadow cast by the steep roof of the house. "Actually, I did hear what you shouted at me, and I thought about it on my journey home. I thought about it as I gathered more shells and sharks' teeth. I thought about it as I came up the river this year, and I decided you were right. I was a fool. You are the right sister for me."

He smiled at her and opened his hand. The rising sun lit up the beautiful pearl that he held there. But she didn't notice that. She only saw that his face was happy again.

QUESTIONS TO CONSIDER

1. Why has Sparrow been crying?

2. What was the city of Cahokia like at the time of this story?

3. What clues do you find in the story that tell you Cahokia was an important city?

4. What was the purpose of the circle of posts at Cahokia?

5. What did you learn about trade in Cahokia from this story?

6. Why is this story called "The Wrong Sister"? Who is the wrong sister?

Cricket Sings:
A Novel of Pre-Columbian Cahokia
by Kathleen King

Kathleen King's story is about a herb-woman and storyteller named Cricket Sings who lives in Cahokia. This exciting tale creates a vivid picture of what life in the ancient city must have been like.

Cahokia: City of the Sun
by Claudia Gellman Mink

This is an informative and beautifully illustrated introduction to life in ancient Cahokia. The book also shows how archaeological research is done at the Cahokia site today.

Prehistoric People of North America
by Diana Childress

Diana Childress tells us what is known about the different peoples who lived in North America from the Ice Age to the arrival of Europeans around A.D. 1500.

The Anasazi Prepare for Company

BY JUDITH LLOYD YERO

Johnny Tafoya burrowed beneath his covers, his mind filled with the wonderful stories he'd heard at tonight's fire. Johnny lived at the **Acoma Pueblo**. At special times, the people gathered around the fire to hear the tales of the old days. Johnny really loved the legends about where his people had come from. Long ago, they had lived deep within the earth. Over time, they moved upward through different levels of the spirit world. Finally, they reached the surface through a hole in the ground—a **sipapu**.

People and Terms to Know

Acoma Pueblo (AH•kuh•muh PWEH•bloh)—village on top of a mesa (flat-topped mountain) in what is now New Mexico. The Acoma are known for their beautiful white pottery decorated in black. Pueblo refers to an Indian community characterized by buildings of adobe. Pueblos are found in the southwestern United States.

sipapu (SEE•pah•poo)—in Pueblo cultures, a small hole in the floor of a special room. The hole represents the place where the Anasazi ancestors came out from inside the earth.

A modern artist's idea of the inside of a kiva. (See page 73.)

Guided by __kachinas__ who came from the spirit world to help them, the people began to look for a sacred place to live.

Johnny yawned. What, he wondered sleepily, would it have been like to live in those times?

*   *   *

In the wink of an eye, Johnny found himself in a strange and wonderful place. Delicious smells rose from dozens of cooking fires on the floor of a great canyon. Sandstone walls rose steeply from the canyon floor. People scurried up and down stairs carved into the stone walls, and the floor of the canyon was busy with activity.

His feet were covered in sandals made of yucca.

Johnny knew that he was no longer in his own time. He wore a simple garment woven of plant fibers. His feet were covered in sandals made of __yucca__. Everything looked different; yet Johnny understood what everyone was doing and why. They were preparing for the great gathering.

People and Terms to Know

__kachinas__ (kah•CHEE•nahz)—supernatural beings that, according to the Pueblo myths, taught and guided their ancestors. (See page 145.)

__yucca__ (YUH•kuh)—plant whose tough fibers were used to weave sandals and to sew animal skins together.

Perhaps later, he would figure out what had happened. Right now, there was too much to see, to do, and to learn.

Soon, visitors would be arriving. The men of the pueblo were adding rooms to the largest stone buildings so that the visitors would have a place to stay. Some of the buildings rose to three or four stories.

Other men hunted for game. Then they dried and smoked the meat over fires. The women ground corn and baked breads. They gathered berries, seeds, and nuts. A few women worked at large looms, weaving robes for the cold days of winter. Strips of rabbit fur were wrapped around the woven cords for warmth. Others scraped the hides of deer, elk, and mountain sheep. Later, they would sew them together with threads made of plant fibers.

Each family group had its own pueblo—up to a dozen small rooms with an open courtyard to the south, a fire pit, a **kiva**, and a trash dump. The

---

People and Terms to Know

kiva (KEE•vah)—Hopi word referring to a circular room that is below ground. Early peoples lived in these pit houses. Later, they were used by family groups for meetings, rituals, storytelling, the instruction of children, and the making of tools and clothing.

rooms were used mainly for storage. The people preferred to spend their time outside. The kiva, often below ground, was used for ceremonies and family activities. Family members would climb down a ladder and sit on stone benches around the outer wall of the circular room. Smoke from the fire rose through the hole in the roof. Fresh air entered from a side tunnel. Each kiva had a sipapu so that the spirits could visit if they wished.

Johnny stopped looking around when he heard a woman's voice scolding him. Her words sounded very much like the language of his own people.

"Lazy boy! Pick up that basket and get to work!"

Johnny reached for the deep and beautifully woven basket at his feet. He grinned at the woman, who pointed toward the distant fields where corn and other crops grew. Johnny took off running. At the fields, the men filled his basket with ears of corn. Johnny followed some other boys back to the buildings, past storage rooms filled with corn, squash, beans, grain, and dried meats.

After emptying his basket, Johnny went back outside. He watched a woman add hot stones to a pottery bowl. The stew of vegetables, squirrel meat, and herbs in the bowl started to boil, sending up fragrant steam. Johnny's stomach growled, but he knew that he had more baskets to carry before he would be allowed to eat.

Over the next few days, people arrived from every direction. Some came from the west, bringing shells and other goods that were unknown to the Pueblo people. Strange people from mysterious lands to the south brought fantastic birds with bright feathers of red, yellow, blue, and green. Others arrived from the north, traveling the miles of roads that connected more than 70 different villages. Most villages had no more than 2,500 people—family groups that joined together to farm and hunt for the good of everyone. The villages

▲
Remains of the Pueblo city at Mesa Verde in Colorado.

grew no larger. People knew that with more people, there would be serious problems.

News was exchanged. Trading for food, clothing, and other goods continued. Johnny eagerly awaited the nightly activities when events were held in the great kiva of __Casa Rinconada__. The great kiva was much larger than the family kivas. Hundreds of people, wearing decorations of __turquoise__, shell, and bone, entered the domed circle, filling the benches along the walls. As the holy men lit the fire, the crowd grew silent. The holy men chanted, and suddenly a man dressed as a kachina appeared, as if by magic, in the center of the floor.

As the holy men lit the fire, the crowd grew silent.

Having explored the kiva during the day, Johnny knew about the underground passage leading to the center of the kiva. But seeing the

---

People and Terms to Know

__Casa Rinconada__ (KAH•sah RIHN•koh•NAH•dah)—large ceremonial kiva in the Chaco Canyon complex in what is now northwestern New Mexico. It was more than 60 feet in diameter and was partly underground. The flat roof was several feet above the ground and was supported by 4 pillars inside the structure.

__turquoise__—greenish blue mineral often used as a gem.

---

feathered figure appear from the smoke, accompanied by sounds of drums and flutes, was still thrilling. It was like watching the spirits coming into the world through the sipapu.

The hard work of the day and steady beat of the drums made Johnny sleepy. Not now, he thought! I have to stay awake and see what happens next!

* * *

"Johnny! Time to get up. You'll be late for school."

Johnny climbed slowly from his bed, knowing that his visit to the world of his ancestors had ended. But he could return at any time—in his imagination.

* * *

The ancient people described in this story were called the **Anasazi**. They lived in present-day Utah, Colorado, New Mexico, and Arizona and produced fine baskets, pottery, cloth, ornaments, and tools.

People and Terms to Know

Anasazi (AH•nah•SAH•zee)—Navajo word meaning "ancient people" or "ancient enemies." The Anasazi were a group of Native Americans who settled in the southwestern region of the United States. Their culture went through several stages beginning about A.D. 100.

Some lived under rock overhangs, like the cliff dwellings of Mesa Verde. Other early Anasazi lived in covered pits dug into the ground. Later, these pits became the kivas used for ceremonies.

The pueblo described in the story is in **Chaco Canyon**, one of the greatest Anasazi settlements. By about A.D. 1000, Chaco was the economic center of the area. But it didn't last. By A.D. 1300, the people had disappeared. Archaeologists argue about why they left. Drought, fewer natural resources such as water and game, attacks by unfriendly non-Pueblo groups, and arguments among themselves may have caused them to leave.

The Anasazi didn't disappear all of a sudden, as some suggest.

The Anasazi didn't disappear all of a sudden, as some suggest. Some groups moved east to the Rio Grande. There they became the Pueblo cultures of northeastern New Mexico, such as Taos and Acoma. Others moved into Navajo territory to create the settlements at the Hopi mesas. More Anasazi ruins are found at Zuni.

People and Terms to Know

Chaco Canyon (CHAH•koh KAN•yuhn)—now a national park in northwestern New Mexico, Chaco Canyon was once the site of a major Anasazi settlement.

The Pueblo people today do not call themselves descendants of the Anasazi. The Navajo used that word to describe their "ancient enemies," and it is considered an insult. However, the Pueblo people still share many of the skills and ways of life of their ancient ancestors.

QUESTIONS TO CONSIDER

1. Why do you think Johnny enjoyed hearing the stories about where his people had come from?

2. How did the people in the canyon spend their days?

3. Why did ancient people travel from all directions to come to Chaco Canyon?

4. What happened to the people of the Chaco Canyon by A.D. 1300?

5. What would you have liked the most about living in the days of the Anasazi? What would you have liked the least?

I Have Killed the Deer

This is a song of the Taos Pueblo people, who, like the Acoma, are thought to be descendants of the Anasazi.

> I have killed the deer.
> I have crushed the grasshopper
> And the plants he feeds upon.
> I have cut through the heart
> Of trees growing old and straight.
> I have taken fish from water
> And birds from the sky.
> In my life I have needed death
> So that my life can be.
> When I die I must give life
> To what has nourished me.
> The earth receives my body
> And gives it to the plants
> And to the caterpillars
> To the birds
> And to the coyotes
> Each in its own turn so that
> The circle of life is never broken.

Ancient Empires

The Hero Twins of the Mayan Sacred Ball Game

BY DEE·MASTERS

At the edge of the jungle near their fathers' old practice ball court, the <u>Mayan</u> boys opened the sack that they had just found. It had been hidden in Grandmother's house. Xbalanque (sh•bah•LAHN•kay) pulled out a solid rubber ball. It was about eight inches thick and weighed about seven pounds.

"What is it?" Hunahpu (hoo•nah•POOH) asked his brother.

People and Terms to Know

Mayan—of or belonging to the Native American people whose ancient civilization in Central America reached its peak from A.D. 300–900 in Mexico, Belize, Guatemala, and parts of El Salvador and Honduras. Mayan people continue to live in these lands today.

Mayan ball players were important figures during the heyday of the Mayan culture. This stone figurine shows a ball player in action.

"It is a **pok-a-tok** ball, oh stupid brother," Xbalanque shot back.

Hunahpu glared at his brother, "I know that! But why was it hidden?"

"Look here," Xbalanque pointed at the sack.

"It's our father's mark! So this must be . . ."

"The pok-a-tok ball our father used when he and our uncle played ball in the **Courts of Creation**," said Xbalanque, finishing his brother's sentence.

"I think I know why we haven't seen it before," said Hunahpu.

"Why, wise one?" his brother asked.

"Grandmother believes pok-a-tok killed our father and our uncle. She does not wish us to play."

"Mother, who came from the great city, says it was the **Lords of Death** who killed them and destroyed our family's honor," Xbalanque replied quietly. "But there is more in the sack." He pulled out two sets of gloves and leather pads. The twins stared at these reminders of their famous father and uncle.

People and Terms to Know

pok-a-tok—Mayan ball game that had religious meaning as well as entertainment value.

Courts of Creation—in Mayan culture, the universe.

Lords of Death—Mayan gods of the underworld. Each represented a form of death.

Finally, Xbalanque broke the silence, "This is a message. Our father and uncle are calling us to the game."

Hunahpu stared at him, "To die at the hands of the Lords of Death in the great city?"

"No! To avenge Father's and Uncle's deaths and win back our family's honor," his brother answered quickly. "Our mother has taught us their tricks. We will win!"

"Well, we won't win if we can't play. First, we have to clear the practice court," Hunahpu commanded. "Only stubble and thistle have played there since our father and uncle died."

They would need more than strength in the great city.

The boys cleared the court and began practicing. Grandmother was not happy. Mother saw that working in the cornfields had made the twins strong and hard. However, they would need more than strength in the great city.

The boys practiced hard at the great game. As they grew stronger and more skillful, so grew their fame until it reached the city and the Lords of Death. The Lords were not pleased. "You must come to play the game against us in seven days," the Lords commanded. They were angry that these farm boys, whose father and uncle had annoyed them, had become so famous. The Lords did not wish to lose control of the game of life.

Grandmother cried, "It is just as it happened before! First my sons and now my grandsons."

"We are not dead yet, Grandmother," the young men assured her. "We have the knowledge our mother gave us. We will restore our family's honor. We will return." The twins traveled to the great city. They made their way through the great market where peasants arrived with loads of salt, tobacco, corn, **cacao**, turkeys, and **jade**. The twins passed through the Gateway of the Nobles and onto a great paved road, eighty feet wide, with painted pyramids rising on either side.

"Mother has told us about all of this," whispered. Hunahpu to his brother, "but it is bigger in real life than it seemed in her stories."

"Have courage, brother. We have come to play the game and win back our honor."

"That we can do!" his brother replied, smiling.

People and Terms to Know

cacao (kuh•KOW)—South American tree used in making cocoa and chocolate.

jade—gemstone that is usually green or white.

"Don't forget how these Lords tricked our father and uncle," Xbalanque reminded Hunahpu.

"Yes," said Hunahpu, "they made fun of our father because he addressed the fanciest dressed Lord as if he were the leader."

"But it was just a dummy made of wood."

"Mother said they laughed hard at our father."

"We are the twins arrived to play pok-a-tok as you commanded."

Xbalanque pointed at the Lords seated on their raised platform. "Look! That Lord has been bitten by a mosquito and brushes it away."

"And those do the same, but not the two on the thrones in the center. They are the wooden ones!" The twins smiled at each other.

Xbalanque shouted, "We are the twins arrived to play pok-a-tok as you commanded."

Xbalanque stared at the real Lords and the wooden Lords and asked loudly, "What's this? Wooden dummies to meet us?" The crowd laughed, but not at the brothers. The Lords' trick had failed.

"Sit down!" one of the Lords demanded, pointing to a stone seat. The two brothers smiled at each other again. Their mother's stories had told them that this special stone seat was burning hot.

The Mayan ball court had an "I" shape, with circular stone goals on each side.

Hunahpu answered, "We thank you, but would prefer not to get a hot seat. It might keep us from playing the game." The Lords were very angry. How did these uneducated country boys know their tricks?

At the ball court the crowd was excited! Many made bets. Many of the bets were made by throwing jewelry onto the court. Some gamblers even bet themselves into slavery. Hunahpu whispered to his brother, "This is much bigger than any court we have played on!" It was 150 feet long and 50 feet wide, in the shape of a capital *I*. The narrow center connector had sloping stone walls. Near the top of each wall was a small stone ring, barely a finger's width bigger than the ball.

The Lords removed their court masks and robes to prepare for the game. They were a scary sight, with their full-body tattoos, their teeth filed to sharp points, and foreheads that had been flattened by boards when they were young.

The game would be decided only by passing the ball through the ring!

The Lords insisted that no score would be kept. The game would be decided only by passing the ball through the ring! The Lords of Death threw their ball first toward Hunahpu's ring. Since no player can touch the ball with his hands or feet, he blocked it with his chest! The Lords of Death angrily drew their knives and moved toward Hunahpu.

Xbalanque shouted, "Lords! Friends of the game! What is happening? The first throw and you wish to kill us? I thought you wanted to play the game. Isn't that what you called us to do?" Xbalanque looked around at the crowd.

"Play the game!" the crowd roared. The Lords did not wish to anger the crowd. The twins prepared to escape.

"No, stay!" shouted a Lord. "You may serve your ball." The hard rubber ball bounced wildly around the court, off the sloped walls, blocked by the knee of one player. Gloves, helmets, and pads protected the men as they raced around the court under the hot jungle sun.

One Lord dived to block a ball and was hit in the stomach. His dead body was carried off the court.

Finally, Xbalanque intercepted a pass by butting it with his head up the steep slope. Hunahpu hit it with his shoulder right through the ring!

The twins had won! The pile of clothing and jewelry that had been bet against them at the end of the court was theirs. And, as was the custom, they chased several nobles and took their expensive jewelry.

But the Lords of Death refused to give the victory to the twins. The Lords wanted another game, and when they lost, yet another and another. Each time the Lords tried to kill the twins, and each time the twins tricked the Lords.

Finally, the twins made themselves look like beggars who had a very exciting trick: they destroyed things and then brought them back fixed. The Lords of Death asked them to perform.

In this ballcourt relief sculpture a captive is being led to the sacrifice as part of a religious ritual.

The twins destroyed a house, a dog, and a person. Then they fixed them! The Lords didn't think they could be destroyed. To prove it, they asked the twins to destroy and restore them. The twins destroyed the Lords of Death, but they wouldn't fix them. And so, the Lords of Death no longer controlled the game of life.

Not only did the twins restore their family honor, but, in Mayan legends, the Hero Twins are still paying pok-a-tok to this day. Only now they play it with the sun and moon!

* * *

There are many legends about the adventures of the Hero Twins. If you were to go to Central America today, you could visit ruins of the ancient Mayan empire at Chichen Itza and see the great ball court. To the ancient Maya, the game of pok-a-tok had great religious meaning. It stood for the story of their creation and the game of life. They believed that in the game of life, people try to defeat the Lords of Death, just as the Hero Twins tried to defeat them on the Courts of Creation.

QUESTIONS TO CONSIDER

1. Why had the boys' Grandmother hidden a sack of pok-a-tok equipment?

2. What message did Xbalanque believe the sack contained?

3. What clues in the story tell you that the great city was an important trading community?

4. Why was the ball game important to the Maya?

5. What made the twins heroes?

Gods and Goddesses of the Ancient Maya
by Leonard Everett Fisher

This guide to the major gods of the Maya explains Mayan beliefs about the powers and traits of their gods. The Mayan religion affected beliefs about life, death, war, and peace. The book also describes Mayan sacrifices.

The Corn Grows Ripe
by Dorothy Rhoads

When Tigre's father is hurt, young Tigre must provide for the rest of the family. He will have to grow up quickly to be sure that there is enough food after the next harvest. The food is not for the family alone—the gods must receive their sacrifice.

Mummy's Home Town— The Curse of the Amulet
by Heather Langlais

Rachel Dubois moves to Mexico with her parents, who are archaeologists. It's very hard for her, especially since she moves so often when her parents begin work at new sites. Maybe her good luck charm will help, or maybe not.

The Legend of Quetzalcoatl

BY MARY KATHLEEN FLYNN

So many times I have heard the story of <u>Quetzalcoatl</u>, the ancient god-king of Mexico, that I can tell it in my sleep. Few people know that, in fact, I had a small part in it.

When I was a little girl, I lived in Quetzalcoatl's spectacular palace in the city of <u>Tula</u>. My parents were personal servants of the great king. Quetzalcoatl himself designed many of the beautiful buildings in the city, as well as the palace. I still remember the palace walls: they were covered with

---

People and Terms to Know

Quetzalcoatl (keht•sa•koh•AT•ihl)—high priest and ruler of the Toltecs, who named himself after the Feathered Serpent god. Legend says that he flashed into the heavens and became the morning star, promising to return one day to rule again.

Tula—capital of Quetzalcoatl's empire. Located about fifty miles northwest of present-day Mexico City, Tula was a beautiful city with great buildings.

Quetzalcoatl wears a skull headdress in this stone sculpture.

This stone sculpture at Tula stands 15 feet tall. ▶

gold, precious jewels, seashells, and colorful bird feathers. Each night I fell asleep to the sweet sounds of birds singing.

Quetzalcoatl was a good and gentle ruler with many talents. He seemed to improve everything he touched. He taught our people, the **Toltecs**, how to grow corn in stunning colors—oranges, reds, browns, and yellows. He invented a calendar and taught us to read and write.

People and Terms to Know

Toltecs—tribe that conquered the central valley of Mexico around A.D. 900, led by Quetzalcoatl's father.

Quetzalcoatl was not just our king but also our priest. He had named himself after the god he prayed to, who was also called Quetzalcoatl. The name means "Feathered Serpent." Other gods wanted human hearts as sacrifices, but the god Quetzalcoatl wanted only small offerings, like butterflies or snakes. Our King Quetzalcoatl, who followed this life-loving god, also loved life and peace.

> *Quetzalcoatl was not just our king but also our priest.*

Quetzalcoatl ruled well for nearly twenty years. But, as in any kingdom, there were those who hated him. He had enemies who prayed to **Tezcatlipoca**, a very powerful god of darkness. Most people think that somehow Tezcatlipoca made Quetzalcoatl give up his kingship.

Tezcatlipoca's name means "Smoking Mirror." It is said that he showed the king a mirror, and when Quetzalcoatl looked into the mirror he saw himself as a very old man. This made Quetzalcoatl think

---

People and Terms to Know

Tezcatlipoca (tesh•kat•lee•POH•kah)—powerful and evil god who loved war. His name means "Smoking Mirror."

about how he would die one day, and he became very sad and scared. It took his confidence away and made it hard for him to rule.

Another rumor I heard was that Tezcatlipoca had tricked Quetzalcoatl into drinking an evil potion made of cactus juice. It made the king drunk, causing him to break his priestly vows. When the king woke up, he was horrified at his own behavior. He felt that he had disgraced himself, and that he no longer had the right to rule his people.

My father and the other men marked the way by shooting arrows into small trees.

No one knows *why* Quetzalcoatl decided to leave Tula, but I can tell you *how* he left, because my parents and I followed our king on his journey.

I'll never forget the night we left the palace and the city of Tula forever. My mother told me we were going to a holy city and that we had to travel down the river to the sea on a raft made of serpents. I was terrified, but my father reminded me that Quetzalcoatl was named after the Feathered Serpent god and that the serpents would protect us.

There were many things that puzzled me that night—and still puzzle me. My father and the other men marked the way by shooting arrows into small trees. Perhaps they did it to help us find our way back. The arrows went through the trees so that the tree trunk and the arrow formed a sort of cross shape.

Quetzalcoatl looked very handsome that night. He was wearing a coat of beautiful brightly colored bird feathers. His fair skin and golden blonde hair and beard shone in the moonlight, making him look young and powerful once again.

At dawn, as we floated down the river, Quetzalcoatl stood at the front of the raft and said that he would rise into the heavens and become the morning star. He said that he would return one day from the place where the sun rises to take back his throne.

And then something fantastic happened. I know this is hard to believe, but suddenly the king burst into flames. It was as if his body was on fire from the heat of the sun. His ashes turned into birds of all colors. The birds flew high into the sky as if they carried Quetzalcoatl's heart to heaven. I knew then that, as he had promised, Quetzalcoatl had become the morning star.

* * *

Five hundred years later, a Spanish captain named **Hernán Cortés** invaded Mexico, and the legend of Quetzalcoatl was revived. Many of the Spaniards were light-skinned, as Quetzalcoatl had been, and they wore clothes of many colors, like the coat of feathers the ancient king had worn. Cortés and his men wore Christian crosses around their necks, which reminded some of the arrows Quetzalcoatl's men had shot through the trees. Many Mexicans thought Cortés was Quetzalcoatl, come home to rule.

QUESTIONS TO CONSIDER

1. What made Quetzalcoatl a good ruler for the Toltecs?
2. What does this story tell you about life in ancient Mexico?
3. How much of the legend of Quetzalcoatl do you think is fact and how much do you think is myth?
4. How might the legend of Quetzalcoatl have helped Cortés and the Spaniards conquer Mexico?

People and Terms to Know

Hernán Cortés—(c. 1485–1547) Spanish captain who conquered Mexico in the 1500s.

The Emperor and the Hummingbird

BY STEPHEN CURRIE

The sun had just risen, but already Itzcoatl (its•koh•AH•tihl) was sweating as he lay curled on his sleeping mat. He yawned and turned over.

"Itzcoatl? Time to get up! Your sister is already in the garden!"

"Yes, Mother." Itzcoatl uncurled, stood, and stretched. He had grown a lot during the last year, and the mat was far too small now. His back felt stiff and sore. Slowly, he stood up, almost tripping over his too-big feet.

"Itzcoatl! Your father is cleaning the streets. It's his work day, and the garden—"

"Coming, Mother!" Every Aztec man had to give several days a year to do work in **Tenochtitlán**:

People and Terms to Know

Tenochtitlán (tehn•ahch•teet•LAHN)—center of Aztec life and government, now Mexico City.

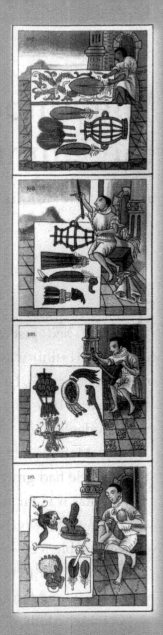

cleaning the streets, building new temples, digging canals. With his father out working, Itzcoatl and his sister would tend the garden this morning. Itzcoatl tied his cloak around his shoulders. He put on his sandals, which had become too small for him. Sandals, a cloak, and a loincloth were all any Aztec man or boy wore in public.

Smiling at his mother, he joined his sister in the garden.

* * *

There was something about a sunny day that filled Itzcoatl with peace. The other houses and gardens of the **calpulli** stretched out in front of him. The calpulli was the center of family life; it was where your neighbors were, your family, your friends. Itzcoatl realized that he had seldom been beyond the borders of his own calpulli. Maybe someday, he thought, but then again there was no need. Everyone and everything he loved was right here.

Still, there was a great world beyond the calpulli. Tenochtitlán was huge; it had a quarter of a million people, perhaps more. Gardens, streets,

People and Terms to Know

calpulli—section of an Aztec city; neighborhood.

markets, houses marched off in all directions. In the distance Itzcoatl could see the city's great temple, and behind that two **volcanoes**. The morning sun glinted off the water of the city's many **canals**. *This is my calpulli, my city, my world*, thought Itzcoatl with pride.

This is my calpulli, my city, my world, thought Itzcoatl with pride.

Breathing deeply in the fresh air, he plucked a ripe ear of corn. His mouth watered. Soon his mother would turn the corn into cornmeal cakes, which they would eat with the peppers and tomatoes picked by his younger sister Atototl (ah•toh•TAH•tihl). He could hardly wait. These days he could not seem to get enough to eat—

"Atototl!" he cried. "You're supposed to be picking!"

Atototl was looking at the bright flowers that sprang up between the rows of vegetables. "Come here," she said softly.

People and Terms to Know

volcanoes—cone-shaped hills or mountains. The volcanoes near Tenochtitlán are Popocatepetl (POH•poh•kah•TEH•peht•uhl), which means "smoking mountain," and Iztacihuatl (ees•tah•SEE•wat•uhl), which means "sleeping woman."

canals—manmade waterways used to water fields or for shipping or travel. Over the years, Aztecs built many roads and bridges to connect the island city to the mainland.

Itzcoatl hurried to her side, tripping over his feet and crushing a flower into the dirt. "What?" he asked.

"A hummingbird." Atototl kept her voice low.

"So?" Hummingbirds were in the garden every day, their tiny wings beating furiously as they drank nectar from the blossoms. Itzcoatl liked to look at the hummingbirds, but what was so wonderful about this one? He leaned down from his new great height. "It looks like any old hummingbird."

"Yes," Atototl said, and she frowned at Itzcoatl. "Only this one *spoke* to me."

* * *

Later that day, Itzcoatl and Atototl were walking along the road to the great market at Tlatelolco (TLAY•teh•LOHL•koh). "What do you mean, the Emperor's life is in danger?" Itzcoatl demanded. He carried some of the rabbit-hair cloth his mother had woven, and Atototl lugged a basket with more. They would sell what they could and buy some items that they needed at home. You could buy almost anything at the market, things from all over Mexico—knives, cloaks, jewels, cocoa, peppers of every kind you could imagine.

"That's what the hummingbird told me," Atototl murmured.

"The hummingbird," Itzcoatl repeated. He pushed her, knocking them both off balance. "You lie." But he wondered. Hummingbirds were special creatures in Tenochtitlán. In an earlier life they had been warriors who had died bravely in battle. Because they had made this sacrifice, they came back to earth to live forever among the flowers.

If the emperor was in danger, what could anyone do?

And Atototl? Itzcoatl stepped onto a bridge over one of the canals that crossed the city. His sister's birth had taken place on a date and at a time that often produced wizards. Sometimes she saw things that no one else saw. He thought back to the earthquake, when the falling house had crushed that man from their calpulli. The day before, Atototl had seen violence in the man's future.

Itzcoatl stumbled as he came off the bridge and onto another smooth wide street. He shook his head, wondering about the emperor and the hummingbird. He had never even laid eyes on the emperor. If the emperor was in danger, what could anyone do?

* * *

The man in the marketplace had been examining Itzcoatl's rabbit-hair cloth. "Too much," he said, dropping the cloth back into the basket.

"That's the price," Itzcoatl murmured. The man had clear eyes and a fine obsidian knife buckled at his side. Probably the man did not belong to their calpulli, Itzcoatl thought. Perhaps he was not even an Aztec. He spoke with an accent of some kind.

"Too much," repeated the man, and he vanished into the crowd.

Itzcoatl sighed. The price was fair, he knew. He stood and stretched. It had been a long afternoon.

"The emperor isn't here," he said to Atototl.

"Yet," said his sister softly.

Itzcoatl snorted. He shut his eyes and listened to the noise of the market around him, a busy hum like the buzz of bees or the sound of waves on the lake. Again, he thought how much he loved Tenochtitlán.

Suddenly Atototl poked him in the ribs. "Look!" she exclaimed.

Itzcoatl's eyes snapped open. There, coming down the broad street, was a procession of guards in fine cloaks, wearing brightly colored feathers on their heads. "The emperor!" someone exclaimed, and the words echoed their way down the row of stalls at the market: "The emperor!" "The emperor!"

The guards passed by slowly, and then there appeared the most amazing sight Itzcoatl had ever seen. It was a man in jewels that shone bright as the sky. He was dressed in a cloak decorated all over with suns, and he carried a bunch of flowers so beautiful they took Itzcoatl's breath away. He walked slowly, his head shielded from the sun by a canopy stretched between several servants.

There was a sudden hush. The people of the calpulli moved back. Only Itzcoatl stayed put. His

Montezuma surrounded by deputies and servants.

eyes could see only the great emperor, *his* emperor, the emperor of all Tenochtitlán.

"Move *back*," insisted Atototl. Embarrassed, Itzcoatl turned to scurry back to her side.

But at the same time there was another cry. "Look out! He has a knife!"

Then everything happened at once. It was the clear-eyed man who had complained about the price of Itzcoatl's cloth. He sprang forward from behind Itzcoatl, his obsidian knife pointed straight for the emperor's chest. The guards reached for their swords. The emperor flinched. Atototl gasped.

And Itzcoatl, hurrying to move back, tripped over his feet and fell heavily onto the shoulder of the man with the knife.

Maybe, he thought a moment later as he, the man, and the knife all clattered to the ground, maybe it was a good thing he had become so tall and clumsy during the last year.

*   *   *

"So you were right," said Itzcoatl as he and Atototl trudged home from the market. "The emperor *was* in danger."

"The hummingbird told me," Atototl reminded him.

"And I saved him." Itzcoatl climbed onto the bridge. "Even if it was an accident, I saved him."

"The hummingbird said the emperor could be saved by a brave young man." Atototl turned to him. "I didn't tell you that part. I suppose that meant you."

A brave young man, thought Itzcoatl. He had never thought of himself that way. But why not? He was sure he *would* have been brave, if he'd had the chance. After all, if the hummingbird said he was brave, it must be true. He lifted his chin, strutted forward like a warrior—

And tripped over his feet, fell off the bridge, and landed with a splash in the canal.

QUESTIONS TO CONSIDER

1. Why were Itzcoatl and Atototl tending the garden on the day of the story?

2. Why were hummingbirds special in the Aztec world? What does this tell you about Aztec values?

3. How did the people in the market react to seeing the emperor? What does that tell you about the emperor's role in Aztec society?

4. According to the story, what goods and ideas were especially important in Aztec culture? What goods and ideas are most important in your culture?

The Aztec Market

Bernal Diaz, one of the Spaniards who invaded Mexico in 1519, was astounded at his first sight of the great Aztec market at Tlatelolco.

Let us begin with the dealers in gold, silver, and precious stones, feathers, cloaks, and embroidered goods, and male and female slaves who are also sold there. . . . There were chocolate merchants with their chocolate. . . . In another part were skins of jaguars and lions, otters, jackals, and deer, badgers, mountain cats, and other wild animals, some untanned, and other classes of merchandise. . . . If I describe everything in detail I shall never be done.

Pachacuti, Inca Empire Builder

BY WALTER HAZEN

My emperor's name meant "destroyer." And it is true that he was sometimes just that. He could lay cities to waste and slaughter their people. Sometimes he even brought the children of captured chiefs to **Cuzco** to make certain his new subjects obeyed.

Do you think that the Supreme Inca **Yupanqui** Pachacuti was just a conqueror of peoples? Let me tell you about him. My emperor was more than just a destroyer. He was also a builder—a great builder. I often stand here looking down at the valley

---

People and Terms to Know

Cuzco—name of both the capital city of the Incas and the valley in which their civilization developed.

Yupanqui (yoo•PANG•kwee)—Inca ruler credited with founding the Inca Empire; also known as Pachacuti (PA•chah•KOO•tee).

The Inca Pachacuti

below, thinking of him and this wonderful monument of his: **Machu Picchu**. He was very proud of this mountaintop city, which can support itself without any outside help. Its rows of **terraces** on the steep slopes below have more than enough food to feed the city's people. But wait—I am ahead of my story. I will tell you more about this great place later.

Some say that he was cruel to destroy cities and their peoples.

Yupanqui, my lord, became the Inca emperor in 1438. (I joined his court at the same time, as an advisor.) "Inca" is the name applied to both our people and our ruler. When Yupanqui followed his father as ruler, he took the name "Pachacuti," which means "destroyer." He had his reasons for choosing this name, as you will see.

Pachacuti soon began to extend his empire by taking over other kingdoms. Some say that he was cruel to destroy cities and their peoples. But he did

---

People and Terms to Know

Machu Picchu—fortress/city built high in the Andes Mountains of what is now Peru.

terraces—series of flat areas cut from slopes that are used for planting. Terraces at Machu Picchu were used for control of erosion (washing away of the soil), for farming, and for ornamental gardens.

this only when his enemies resisted his rule. Most of the time he did not have to destroy the enemy because people knew that Pachacuti treated conquered peoples fairly. If they swore to be loyal to him, he treated them the same as the Incas. He even gave his former enemies high jobs in his government.

Because I was a close advisor to Pachacuti, he often asked me to take a special message to the chief of a city he planned to attack. I remember the first time I took this message to a ruler. I said to the ruler's advisor:

"My emperor states that if your city surrenders and does not resist, all its people will be given the same rights as we Incas. Everyone will have the protection of the Inca, and, in times of need, everyone will have plenty of food to eat."

"And if my lord chooses not to give in?" the enemy advisor said.

"Then," I continued, "you can expect no pity from the great Pachacuti. He will either kill your leading families or haul them off to our awful prison in Cuzco. Our prisons are filled with poisonous snakes and wild animals."

I don't need to tell you that many enemy chiefs gave up without a fight! Yes, our prisons are terrible places. It is no surprise that, for the most part, they remain almost empty. Wouldn't you think twice about committing a terrible crime if you knew you would be locked up with snakes?

My emperor had a strong belief in justice. He was very severe on dishonest judges. One day he said to me, "Judges who take bribes are thieves and deserve death."

And they were killed. They were not thrown into a prison with poisonous snakes and wild animals, but they suffered almost as badly. I have seen dishonest judges and nobles either stoned to death or hanged by their feet until they died. I have seen others thrown from cliffs or beaten to death with clubs. Did I pity them? No. In my humble opinion, they got what they deserved.

In spite of his strictness, I believe that Pachacuti will be remembered more for what he built than for what he destroyed. One of his greatest achievements was Machu Picchu. The city sits near the top of a mountain about 7,000 feet up. It will serve as a strong fortress against attack for many years to come. My emperor was proud of the way the fortress was built. Stones used in the buildings fit so closely together that one cannot insert a knife between them. Stairways chiseled into the mountain connect temples, homes, and other structures.

And **aqueducts** supply the people with plenty of fresh water. Beautiful fountains are everywhere in the city. The city is a wonder to see.

Pachacuti was also proud of Cuzco, our capital. When he became emperor, Cuzco was little more than an enclosed village. Its houses were built of sod or sun-dried brick, with roofs made of thatch or straw. Pachacuti changed all that. Before his rule ended, he turned Cuzco into a great city.

Our emperor laid the city out in the shape of a **puma**. He did that because the puma is an important animal in our religion. As for our city's streets, they cross in the pattern of a **trapezoid**. This means they do not cross at right angles. Even the doors and windows of houses are trapezoids. The trapezoid pattern is a favorite of our architects and engineers.

It is the Huacaypata, (HWA•kay•PAH•tah) or great square, for which our city is famous. Here, Pachacuti built temples and other royal buildings. Here, too, are the palaces of the Inca and the houses of the nobles, as well as various government offices.

People and Terms to Know

aqueducts—large stone structures through which water flows from mountainous areas into cities.

puma—large wildcat found in many parts of North and South America.

trapezoid—four-sided figure having two sides that are parallel and two sides that are not.

All the buildings are made of solid stone, and the most important are plated with sheets of gold. From the distance, they gleam in the sunlight. A person approaching from the distance thinks at first that the city is made of gold!

> *All the buildings are made of solid stone, and the most important are plated with sheets of gold.*

As the Inca's advisor, I saw how he created our wonderful empire. When he became the Supreme Inca, the territory we controlled was small. It consisted mostly of Cuzco and the nearby area. Through war, Pachacuti extended our boundaries so that they stretched for some 2,000 miles. In doing so, he built a long line of fortresses along our eastern frontier. The greatest of these was Machu Picchu.

As our empire grew, Pachacuti made sure that it was connected by a good system of roads. Our army and our swift postal runners travel over these roads. Our postal runners can relay messages as far as 150 miles in one day. This is quite amazing since some mountain passes are more than three miles high.

The ruins of the city of Machu Picchu in the Andes Mountains of Peru.

Do you think that the Supreme Inca Yupanqui Pachacuti was just a conqueror of peoples and a builder of empires and cities? Then let me set the record straight. The Inca was also a deep thinker and a person of great wisdom. Once, while we were discussing how to judge a person's character, he said: "The noble and generous man is known by the patience he shows in hard times."

Well put, if I must say so myself, and I believe that my emperor lived his life according to these values. I have lived many years beyond Inca Yupanqui's death. During this time, I have thought much of his reign and his achievements. Don't you agree, now, that my emperor was a great and wise ruler?

QUESTIONS TO CONSIDER

1. Why do you think Yupanqui took a name that meant "destroyer"?

2. How did he treat the people he conquered who offered no resistance?

3. Why were the prisons of the Incas such terrible places?

4. What made the great square of Cuzco a great place?

5. What present-day leaders act similarly to Yupanqui? Give examples.

Machu Picchu: The Story of the Amazing Inkas and Their City in the Clouds
by Elizabeth Mann

One of the most sacred places of the Incan Empire was discovered less than 100 years ago! This book gives a tour of the ancient city of Machu Picchu, which was built high in the mountains of Peru.

Discovering the Inca Ice Maiden: My Adventures on Ampato
by Johan Reinhard

In 1995, the mummy of a 14-year-old girl was found trapped in ice on the side of the Ampato volcano in Peru. Not only does this book explain how they found the girl, but also what—and who—they found buried on the mountain with her.

Lost Treasure of the Inca
by Peter Lourie

Ready for adventure? This book takes you on a search for the lost gold of the Incan Empire. It includes a map to show you where the riches were left. The secrets of the Incas are always just over the next mountain.

The Story of Malinche

BY JANE LEDER

The story of **Malinche** has many sides. Was she a traitor? A survivor? Or a victim? Each of the following three people presents a different view of her.

* * *

Aztec Woman

I survived the 1521 massacre of my Aztec people by the Spaniard Hernán Cortés and his men. The traitor, Malinche, was the daughter of a noble Aztec family. Because Malinche could speak both our language and the Spanish language, Cortés chose her as his

---

People and Terms to Know

Malinche (mah•LIHN•chay)—Aztec slave woman (c. 1500) who became the translator for Spanish conquistador Hernán Cortés.

Malinche (left) is shown here with Spanish explorer Hernán Cortéz (right).

translator. He depended on her to help him speak with the Aztec people he planned to conquer.

Malinche was the one who told Cortés about our city of Tenochtitlán and about all the gold and other riches we had. If it hadn't been for Malinche, the greedy Cortés might never have come.

Montezuma was the ruler of the Aztecs, and over the years he had made many enemies in the nearby territories. Each time Cortés and his men marched into one of our enemy territories, Malinche would help convince them to join Cortés and fight against us. You see, Malinche no longer believed in our gods. After she joined Cortés, she was baptized and became a Christian.

My people knew nothing about Christianity; we had many gods. One of our gods was Quetzalcoatl, a white-skinned god with a long beard who sailed eastward over the sea a long time ago. We believed he would one day return from the sea to reclaim his power.

This Spaniard, Cortés, had very light skin, a long beard, and hair that came only to his ears.

People and Terms to Know

Montezuma—(c. 1480–1520) last ruler of the Aztec Empire. He ruled from 1502 until his defeat by Cortés's forces.

Montezuma, our king, became convinced that this man was Quetzalcoatl, returned to us. That is why Montezuma welcomed Cortés to our splendid city.

I saw Malinche the day the two men came face-to-face for the first time. I was a young girl at the time, and I thought that Malinche was a proud-looking woman. I hoped and prayed she would be loyal to her people—that she would con-

I hoped and prayed she would be loyal to her people.

vince Cortés not to harm us or to conquer our city. But she betrayed us. Malinche told Montezuma that Cortés had come as a friend and that there was nothing to fear. But in no time at all, Cortés had taken our emperor prisoner.

What a liar he was! And this Malinche, born of Aztec people—what a traitor! Cortés's men fired one of their great cannons. I, with many others, ran off in panic.

Our people tried to fight back with spears and arrows, but we were no match for the iron arrows and the cannons of the strangers.

After eighty days of fighting, a handful of survivors fled from the ruins of our city. Cortés, with the help of Malinche, had won the Aztec Empire.

* * *

Spanish Soldier

I am a soldier who marched alongside Cortés from the shores of Old Mexico to the city of Tenochtitlán. I remember meeting Malinche during our march. I thought she seemed like a very smart and brave woman.

Malinche was one of twenty slaves given to Cortés by a local chief. Cortés gave the women to his captains; Malinche was given to Alonzo Hernando Puertocarrero. Then Cortés discovered that Malinche knew how to speak several local **dialects**. He was no fool. He needed a translator, so he made Puertocarrero his messenger to Spain. Then he took Malinche for himself.

To show her respect for Cortés, Malinche chose to be baptized a Christian, and took the name Doña Marina.

It was from Doña Marina that Cortés first learned of the rich and powerful king, Montezuma, and the fabulous city of Tenochtitlán. Cortés wrote a letter to our emperor in Spain, **Charles V**, promising to conquer the Aztec ruler. Cortés said he

People and Terms to Know

dialects—regional variations of a language.
Charles V—(1500–1558) king of Spain. Cortés conquered Mexico in his name.

would bring back this Montezuma either dead or in chains, if he would not submit himself to Spain.

Moving inland from the coast of Mexico to Tenochtitlán was very hard. We marched through a desert land and we had no water and little food. Native Indians often attacked us and we suffered many losses of men and supplies.

Through it all, Doña Marina was as brave as any man.

Through it all, Doña Marina was as brave as any man. Every day, she heard how the Indians were going to kill us and eat our flesh with chili. She was there as we were surrounded in battle. Yet she never showed any signs of fear, only courage.

Along the way, it was Doña Marina who translated for Cortés, speaking to the Indians in their own languages. Many of these men joined forces with us, more than willing to fight against the evil and greedy Montezuma.

We reached Montezuma's city on November 8, 1519. With Doña Marina at his side, Cortés tricked Montezuma into thinking we had come as friends.

He had scarcely welcomed us when we took him prisoner. His people fought us fiercely for eighty days, but in the end, we finally took full control of Montezuma in the name of His Majesty of Spain.

Montezuma, shown here in a European drawing, holds a spear and a shield. The European artist makes him look almost Roman.

* * *

Modern Mexican

I am a Mexican living close to Mexico City. It has been more than 500 years since the woman we call Malinche lived here.

For the most part, people in today's Mexico see Malinche as a traitor to her people. Yet I find her story very complicated and am not sure what to make of her.

Malinche was born into a wealthy family; some even say she was an Indian princess. She loved her father and spent many hours playing and studying with him. At that time, most girls weren't given a formal education, but the high position of Malinche's family allowed her to go to school. She was a smart young girl who loved languages and loved to please her father.

Malinche's days as a princess came to a sudden end when her father died. Her mother remarried and had another child, a son. Now her mother wanted the son, not Malinche, to inherit the family wealth and position. So she took the young girl in the middle of the night and actually gave her away to slave traders. As far as Malinche's mother was concerned, her daughter was dead.

As a slave, Malinche learned several local dialects and proved herself to be very good with languages. When Hernán Cortés needed slaves for his captains, Malinche was one of the women chosen. Cortés soon took Malinche as his own, and she served her master well, becoming his translator, companion, and mother of one of his children.

After the conquest of Mexico, Cortés returned to his wife in Spain. Before he left, he arranged to have Malinche married to another man.

How could Cortés leave Malinche behind to raise his son? Her heart must have been broken. She must have dreamed of the day when Cortés would return. Cortés died in 1547. Malinche never saw him again.

QUESTIONS TO CONSIDER

1. Why did the Aztecs think Cortés was a god?
2. What part do you think gold played in the Spanish invasion of Mexico?
3. Why do many Mexicans see Malinche as a traitor? Do you think she was a traitor? Explain.
4. What might cause some to portray Malinche as a survivor?
5. What does the story of Malinche show you about how people in history can be remembered?

Many Nations

New Life in Vinland

BY BRIAN J. MAHONEY

In the early dawn light, Gudrid lay in the long grass, staring up at the puffy white clouds in the open sky. "What am I doing here?" she whispered, focusing on a cloud shaped like **Thor's hammer**. She secretly hoped it would descend and level their settlement. She wanted to go home—away from this place. But, she wondered, where was home, after all?

Since leaving **Norway** as a small child, she seemed always to have been traveling west. First, her parents had moved their young family to the

---

People and Terms to Know

Thor's hammer—Thor, a powerful and popular Viking god, was believed to protect the cosmos with a giant hammer.

Norway—country in northern Europe occupying the western and northern parts of the Scandinavian peninsula.

A modern artist imagines a Viking family inside a settlement hut in Vinland.

thriving **Viking** settlement in **Iceland**. Then they had followed **Erik the Red** to his new settlement in **Greenland**. Now, here she was, in **Vinland**, on what seemed to be the very edge of the western world.

Gudrid looked longingly out to sea. Could she return to Greenland? Oh, but Greenland was so cold and barren. It was a place where winter would freeze the ocean solid. It was there that she had married Thorstein, the son of Erik the Red. After Thorstein grew ill and died, Erik had kindly taken her into his household. There she met **Thorfinn**, her new husband.

Gudrid remembered how excited she and Thorfinn had been when Erik's son **Leif** told them

---

People and Terms to Know

Viking—pertaining to fierce, seafaring warriors who terrorized many European areas with their savage raids from the ninth to eleventh centuries. Viking homelands were the Scandinavian countries of Norway, Denmark, and Sweden, in northern Europe.

Iceland—island in the Atlantic Ocean, 620 miles west of Norway and 185 miles east of Greenland. Iceland was settled by Vikings in the ninth century.

Erik the Red—(950–1001) Norse chief, explorer, and colonizer.

Greenland—large island off northeast Canada, lying mostly within the Arctic Circle. Greenland was discovered, named, and settled by the Norse chief Erik the Red in about A.D. 986. According to one of the sagas, he called it Greenland because "people would be attracted to go there if it had a favorable name."

Vinland—"wine land" or "grass land," Leif Eriksson's name for a settlement area in North America.

Thorfinn—(980–c. 1007) Thorfinn Karlsefni, Gudrid's second husband, a wealthy trader from Iceland.

Leif—(975–1020) Leif Eriksson, son of Erik the Red. Leif Eriksson discovered a land he called Vinland in the northern part of North America in about 1000.

about the way he had discovered and named Vinland. Like father, like son! Gudrid and Thorfinn had immediately started making plans to be Vinland's first settlers.

Now, here she was, lying in the grass, staring at the sky, and wishing that she were anywhere else. In many ways, life here was good. It was warmer than Greenland and Iceland, and the sun shone longer

Yet something nagged at her— she didn't feel safe here.

here. There were lakes and rivers teeming with fish, and the land was good for crops. Yet something nagged at her—she didn't feel safe here. Perhaps it was because she knew that they weren't alone in this land.

So far, the settlers hadn't seen any of the native people, but Gudrid couldn't forget that a few years ago the **Skraelings** had killed Leif's brother Thorvald. "We could return to Thorfinn's home in Iceland," she thought. "He could go back to trading, and we could raise a family—and attend a real church!"

People and Terms to Know

Skraelings—Viking term for Native Americans.

Suddenly, something broke through the grass and leaped over her—startling Gudrid. She sprang to her feet, ready to fight, but it was only a deer, running off through the tall grass. The fright seemed to have awakened Gudrid's fighting spirit. She decided that she would not bow to her fears. After all, she was a leader known for her courage and intelligence. She wouldn't let a weak moment ruin what she had accomplished.

Ah, and wouldn't Freydis love to see me admit weakness? thought Gudrid. Freydis believed that, as Erik the Red's daughter and Leif's sister, she and her husband should be the leaders of the expedition, not Gudrid and Thorfinn.

Freydis was always challenging Gudrid. Just last night, when Gudrid suggested that they move their settlement away from the shore to a safer place, Freydis had mocked her and called her a coward. A slow anger rose in Gudrid as she remembered the insults. Her eyes narrowed into a burning glare that shot across the wild wheat field and fixed on Freydis's sod-covered house. She knew what she needed to do—she would set Freydis straight once and for all!

Boom! Boom! Boom! Gudrid pounded on the rough wooden door. "FREYDIS! COME OUT!" The door opened, first revealing a shaking iron dagger, and then the shaking boy that held it. (An old Viking saying warned that one should always open doors prepared for an enemy on the other side.) Nervously, the boy said, "The Skraelings are coming. Everyone went to meet them at the water's edge."

Gudrid went cold. Would the Skraelings attack them, as they had attacked and killed Thorvald? Snatching the dagger, she ran to the shore. An armed crowd had gathered at the water's edge, and over their heads she saw a frightening sight.

Nine rough boats floated opposite them, and in them stood dark men twirling poles that made a loud swishing noise. They wore pieces of animal skin and had broad, lean faces framed with tangled hair.

Gudrid could feel her fellow settlers bracing for attack. Thorfinn's strong voice carried over the swishing sound. "What do you suppose that pole-twirling means?" he asked. His friend Snorri replied, "It may be a sign of peace. We should wave the white shield." They did, and the Skraelings quietly came ashore.

Each group stared at the other. The tall, blue-eyed Vikings towered over their raw-looking visitors. As the two sides signed and motioned their peaceful intentions, the crowd relaxed. Gudrid spotted Freydis's ivory comb bobbing atop her pointy head.

> *The tall, blue-eyed Vikings towered over their raw-looking visitors.*

Their eyes met, and Freydis approached without breaking the stare.

"So nice of you to show up!" Freydis said loudly. "For a moment I thought that we would all meet my brother's bloody end while you hid yourself in the tall grass!" Most of the crowd turned from the Skraelings to watch something more interesting. Gudrid felt their stares as she spoke. "If Erik the Red weren't your father, this dagger would release your black heart of its ugly burden."

* * *

As time went on, Gudrid and Freydis avoided each other. Months passed slowly, and the others took pains to insure that Gudrid and Freydis would not meet in the same room without warning. In summer, the settlers busied themselves with harvesting the land's endless bounty: berries,

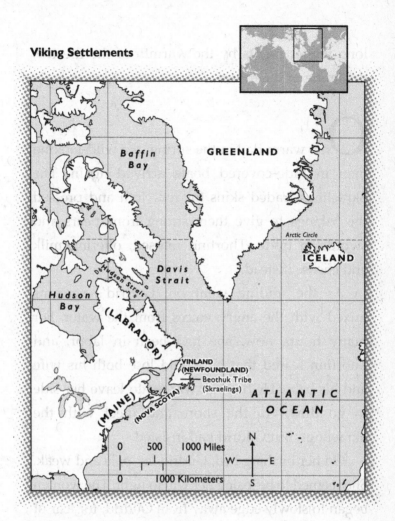

Viking Settlements

Baffin
Bay

GREENLAND

Arctic Circle

ICELAND

Davis
Strait

Hudson Strait

Hudson
Bay

(LABRADOR)

VINLAND
(NEWFOUNDLAND)
Beothuk Tribe
(Skraelings)

ATLANTIC
OCEAN

(MAINE)

(NOVA SCOTIA)

0   500   1000 Miles

0   1000 Kilometers

N
W   E
S

fish, wild grain, and game. The livestock were fat
year-round.

Gudrid and Thorfinn's love grew stronger as
they worked together to build their new life. In the
fall, Gudrid learned that she was expecting a child.
Thorfinn couldn't contain his joy. They passed the

long winter nights by the warmth of the fireside, dreaming of the future.

On a warm day in the spring, the wild-looking men in hide-covered boats arrived again. The Skraelings traded skins for red cloth and pressed the Vikings to give them strong iron spears and swords in trade. Thorfinn refused, offering milk and cheese instead.

As the trading went on, Gudrid's screams mixed with the angry voices from the water. For many hours now, she had been in labor, and Thorfinn feared that he would lose both his wife and his baby. He had not wanted to leave her side to go down to the shore and meet with the Skraelings, but Gudrid had insisted.

On her birthing bed, Gudrid lay pale and weak. She seemed to be losing her will to fight. The women began to slowly edge away from Gudrid, for fear of seeing her death. Gudrid began to pray, "Please Lord, let me give birth to my baby before I die."

At that moment, Gudrid's doorway darkened, and a figure came into the light. Freydis stood there, sword in hand. A strange moment passed. Freydis's figure softened. Finally, she dropped the sword to the floor. "It looks as if, for once, you need my help," said Freydis.

Freydis took charge, screaming orders at the other women and giving directions to Gudrid. Outside, the traders' angry voices became louder. "It sounds as if the Skraelings are getting ready to attack us," said Freydis. "You'd better hurry up with that baby!"

The men outside were also starting to worry about the Skraelings' rising anger. Suddenly, from inside the house came such a loud scream that one of the bulls broke loose from its pen and ran out on the beach toward the traders. The Skraelings, who had never seen such a creature before, took fright, ran to their boats, and quickly paddled away.

Suddenly all was quiet. Like lightning, Thorfinn turned, rushed to the house, and swung open the door, fearing the worst. He was greeted by a most unexpected sight—Freydis and Gudrid in the same room, and both were smiling. They were smiling at the bundle that Gudrid held in her arms. Gudrid looked up at her husband. "Like father, like son!" she said, with a tired shake of her head. "This is Snorri, Thorfinn—and you're both late." Thorfinn's smile lit the room as his son's blue eyes opened and looked at the New World around him.

QUESTIONS TO CONSIDER

1. Who is Gudrid, and why did she come to Vinland?

2. What was life like for Viking women?

3. Who were the Skraelings, and how did they first approach the Viking settlers on their land?

4. What qualities made a good Viking?

5. How did the Vikings view the Skraelings? How do you view them and why might your view be different from the Vikings'?

6. What seem to have been the advantages and disadvantages for the Vikings of life in Vinland?

Viking
by Susan M. Margeson

Susan M. Margeson gives an overview of the Vikings' way of life, presenting images of their furniture, clothing, weapons, jewelry, and many other items.

The Vikings
by Elizabeth Janeway

Elizabeth Janeway provides a good general introduction to the world of the Vikings, including their voyages to North America.

Raiders and Traders
by Anita Ganeri

Anita Ganeri's look at a day in the life of Vikings is richly illustrated and gives a thorough introduction to the daily lives of the Vikings.

Hopi Migrations

BY STEPHEN CURRIE

At different times in their history, the Hopi traveled through the southwestern part of what is now the United States. Over many centuries, some Hopi village sites show evidence of having been settled and then abandoned. Hopi pottery and rock markings have been found in parts of the Southwest where Hopi people no longer live.

The Hopi have many legends telling about the early **migrations** of their people. The events described in this story tell some of these tales.

*　　*　　*

People and Terms to Know

migrations—movements of groups of people from place to place.

Hopi kachinas come in many designs and represent different animals, gods, and people. These are on display at the Southwest Museum in Los Angeles.

"Here is the Fourth World," said **Sotuknang**. He stood on the shore that marked the entrance to the new world. His eyes carefully studied the people silently waiting to enter. "The Third World is no more. I have destroyed it, as I destroyed the First World and the Second World. Soon you will step through the entrance and into the new land I have prepared for you."

The people murmured in excitement, eager to see the world that would soon be theirs. Behind them lay the ruins of the Third World. Water covered everything, even the tops of the highest mountains. Sotuknang had sent the water to flood the Third World and make the way for the new one. Several of the young men pushed forward, hoping to be first across the entrance.

"There is one thing I still must say to you," Sotuknang said, and the young men halted in their tracks. "This new world is not like the old ones. In the old worlds, life was always easy, but this Fourth World I give you now is not so easy. It contains both good and bad. It has beauty and ugliness, love and

---

People and Terms to Know

Sotuknang—in Hopi tradition, the nephew of the Creator and the first being created. He organized the universe and directed the creation of the first people, then he gave them speech and wisdom.

hatred, joy and sorrow. This world is a world complete in itself. Make it what you will."

The people were silent.

"To know this world," continued Sotuknang, "you must explore it from north to south and from east to west. Each clan will go its own separate way, four times around the land. You will follow your stars to the spot where you will meet once more and settle."

> *"You will follow your stars to the spot where you will meet once more and settle."*

"Will it be soon?" asked an old woman of the Flute Clan.

"It will not be soon," said Sotuknang. He alone knew how long—he knew that even the youngest of the people would be old well before the migrations were complete. But Sotuknang also knew that the migrations would purify the people and heal them from the evils of the previous worlds.

"One last word," he told them. "Always keep open the **door on the top of your heads**. And now, I wish you well, all of you," and he turned his face

---

People and Terms to Know

door on the top of your heads—The Hopi believed that the earliest human beings were able to communicate with the Creator through soft spots on the tops of their heads.

and became invisible, and the people poured through the doorway into the Fourth World to begin their migrations.

*   *   *

Some clans went to the south. Among them were those of the Parrot Clan. There were only a few people in the Parrot Clan, and they were old. When they arrived in the hot lands of South America, there were so few it seemed as if the clan would surely die out.

Soon they came to a jungle. There an old woman spoke up. "I will walk into this jungle," she said, "and I will search for a power to make us a fertile people and keep our clan alive."

"And I will go with you," said her husband. So the two walked into the jungle. There they met a man who brought them to a fine house where a beautiful woman lived.

"You have prayed for babies," said the beautiful woman, and she smiled at the old couple. "Here in the forest I see all, hear all, know all. I sent my messenger to summon you, for I can tell your wishes are sincere."

In the room there was a nest, such as a parrot or other bird might weave, and in the nest were brightly colored eggs, such as a parrot might lay.

"Put your hand on the eggs," commanded the beautiful woman, "and pray again for what you desire."

The man and the woman did as they were told, and soon they felt the stirrings of new life within the eggs. "That is all," said the beautiful woman. "Return now to your clan, blessed with the power of these eggs. There will be enough babies to carry on the name of the clan. Indeed, other clans seeking to grow will ask for your blessing. Please give them your blessing as I have given you mine."

Soon there was snow everywhere, and their bones felt the bitter chill.

"We shall!" they said. And they did.

* * *

Other clans went north. After many days of travel they found that it began to grow cold. Soon there was snow everywhere, and their bones felt the bitter chill. It might have been wise if they had stopped there and turned to the east, as the stars commanded; but those of the Fire and the Sun Clans used their powers to create heat. And so the people did not stop, but continued northward until at last their way was blocked.

"It is a mountain of snow," said some. "It is a sea of ice," said others, and indeed it was both, and it stretched as far as the eye could see. "This is the back door of the Fourth World," most agreed; "the door is closed to us, and we must turn onto another path."

"You must use your sacred powers only for good."

But those of the Spider Clan wished to continue. "Use your powers on the snow and ice," they said to those of the Fire Clan and the Sun Clan. "Melt the snow and melt the ice, so we may see what lies beyond."

Four times the Fire and Sun Clans tried, and each time they failed. Even the most angry fire and the mighty sun could not melt the ice and snow. At last Sotuknang appeared. "This is the closed back door of the Fourth World," he said. "If you had melted the ice, there would have been a flood which would have changed the shape of this world forever."

Those of the clans did not dare to speak.

"You must use your sacred powers only for good," warned Sotuknang. "Because the Spider Clan tried to melt the ice, from now on the Spider Clan will only be a force for evil. That is what I had to say; now I have said it."

The clans turned to the east, but ever afterwards the Spider Clan could only bring wickedness into the world, and they were cast out by the rest of the people.

*   *   *

And still other clans started their journeys in other directions. Each clan had many adventures. The Badger Clan got its name from a badger who cured a gravely ill girl. The Snake Clan traveled to the prairies and built a mound of earth in the shape of a serpent. The Eagle Clan constructed a great city of stone far to the south.

Across the Americas the people traveled, wandering as the stars guided them. Four times they went around, north, east, south, west; four times they made a circle. As they passed a place, they drew clan **petroglyphs** to show they had been there, and added circles to show how many times.

At last the Bear Clan completed its journey and returned to the center of the Fourth World. There they built a village, and then another, and then another still. One by one the other clans returned.

People and Terms to Know

petroglyphs—carvings in rock; each clan had its own symbol, such as a coyote for the Coyote Clan.

▲
Hopi petroglyphs were symbols chiseled into rocks to tell stories to others.

The migrations were over, and the people had been purified. Once again they could all be together.

But though the journeys were over, the telling of them has never stopped, and it will not stop so long as the Fourth World survives.

*   *   *

The Hopi trace their culture and traditions back to prehistoric peoples such as the Anasazi culture. According to Hopi tradition, the human race has gone through three different stages, or "worlds." Each world has been destroyed because humans became too greedy or evil. The surviving humans are now living in the Fourth World. There are three more worlds to come.

The First World was a paradise that was destroyed by volcanoes. In the Second World, humans learned crafts and lived in huts; this world was destroyed by ice. People in the Third World built cities and tall buildings, which were destroyed by floods. The story you have just read is based on Hopi stories about the Fourth World.

QUESTIONS TO CONSIDER

1. How was the Fourth World different from other worlds?

2. What do you think Sotuknang meant when he said "Always keep open the door on the top of your heads"? How was this concept important to the Hopi?

3. Why do you think Sotuknang was angrier with the Spider Clan than with the Sun or Fire Clans?

4. What does the story of the migrations tell you about the Hopi view of the world? How is it different from your world view? How is it the same?

5. What connections can you make between the first three worlds of the Hopi and the climate changes that actually took place in prehistoric times?

The Taino See Three Ships

BY DANNY MILLER

Atabey was busy grinding kernels of **maize** when she heard loud knocks on the wall of her hut. The girl placed the tool she was using on a wooden shelf that hung from the rafters and walked to the doorway. There she saw her younger brother, Bagua, bouncing a rubber ball against the side of the thatched home they shared with several other families.

"What are you doing, Bagua?" Atabey asked, licking some maize paste off her finger. "I've got a lot of work to do before Mother returns. Why don't you come in and help me?"

People and Terms to Know

maize (mayz)—corn.

"Sorry, sister," the boy said. "Our chief said I could help Father and the other men hunt for tonight's celebration! We're going to look for **iguanas**. Then we're going to the lake to fish and catch geese!" Bagua beamed. He'd waited a long time for this.

"Did the chief say anything more about his vision?" Atabey asked. The whole **Taino** village was talking about what their chief had shared with them at the last **areytos**. He said that the god **Yocahú** had appeared to him and told him there was great trouble ahead for their people. He said that men covered in strange cloth would come to their land and change their lives forever.

"No, he didn't mention it," said Bagua as he started down the path to meet the men. "Everyone thinks the vision is about the **Caribs**. I'm not worried." Atabey did not feel any better. Just then, two brightly colored parrots swooped down toward Bagua, as if to tease the boy, and flew into the hut. Bagua laughed and ran off.

People and Terms to Know

iguanas (ih•GWAH•nuhz)—large tropical lizards.

Taino (TY•noh)—Native American people of a group of tropical islands in the Caribbean, southeast of Florida. San Salvador is the island depicted in this story.

areytos (AHR•ee•YEHT•ohz)—Taino celebration, involving songs and dances.

Yocahú (yoh•ka•HOO)—god worshipped by the Taino.

Caribs—another tribe in the region, enemies of the Taino.

Looking toward the fields, Atabey spotted her mother, walking with a group of women. They were carrying large baskets of freshly picked **cassava** and smaller baskets of yams and papayas. Some of the women held huge bunches of flowers in their arms—oversized buds bursting with reds, yellows, purples, and blues. Gifts for the chief, Atabey thought.

Some of the women held huge bunches of flowers in their arms.

Atabey greeted her mother and helped the women carry the baskets into the hut. Grabbing a piece of chipped flint, the girl joined the women as they peeled away the rough outer skin of the cassava plants. After grating the white flesh, they squeezed it through a finely woven fabric to remove the bitter juices.

The women sang beautiful songs while they worked, songs of their people's history and beliefs. Atabey sang along, passing the grated cassava from one hand to the other and shaping it into a flat disc.

People and Terms to Know

cassava (kuh•SAH•vah)—tropical plant that was a staple of the Taino diet. Also called manioc.

Taino ceremonial axe.

But the thought of the chief's vision was never far from her mind. The women set the dough onto clay griddles, and placed them on hot stones in the fire. After the dough cooked, they put the cassava breads out into the sun to dry.

Later, the men returned and began preparing their fish and game for the feast. Atabey's father waved to her as he set about constructing a grill from green sticks and charcoal. She wanted to talk to him about the vision, but he seemed too busy. She smiled when she saw Bagua jumping up and down near a pile of iguanas that were laid out next to a mound of small but tasty rice rats. Some of the men emptied baskets of oysters and mussels into a pile for sorting.

After the food was prepared, the men and women began to get themselves ready for the festivities. Atabey's mother painted bright designs of black and red markings on her husband. Atabey painted similar designs on Bagua. Everyone in the family wore strings of seashells or small stones. Atabey draped strands of small seashells around her hips and ankles. The shells would make a lovely clinking sound when she danced with the other girls at the areytos. Some of the adults wore gold bands in their noses and around their arms.

The celebration was a huge success. The dance Atabey's group performed told the story of how her people had come to this island. The rest of the villagers copied the steps. When the roasted iguanas were brought out, Bagua made sure everyone knew about his role in the hunt. People shook hollow gourds filled with seeds and played on large wooden drums. Stories of the people's proud history were told and retold.

The chief spoke to the crowd and expressed his thanks. Atabey noticed that he didn't say anything about his vision. In addition to food and flowers, the people presented the chief with several new zemis, small statues of their gods. The zemis were carved out of wood or stone and those given to the chief were very beautiful.

"Monsters! Sea monsters with huge white wings!"

After the celebration, Atabey and her family made their way back to the hut with the others. Each person took out a rolled-up hammock and set it up on wooden posts. Atabey sneaked away and prayed to her zemis, asking them to protect her people.

Early the next morning, Atabey awoke to the cries of the village healer. She ran to the entrance of the hut where her parents and brother already stood.

"Look! Out there!" the healer yelled, pointing to the sea. Atabey's eyes slowly adjusted to the early light of dawn. She couldn't understand what she was seeing. It looked as if three huge birds were coming to their island.

Bagua was thrilled. "Monsters! Sea monsters with huge white wings!" he cried.

Soon most of the people in the village had made their way to the shore to get a better look at the incredible sight. Some hid behind bushes, but others were so curious they waded into the water. Atabey stood on the sand holding Bagua's hand tightly, her parents behind her.

Bagua gazed at the objects, which were getting closer. "I see men standing on the winged monsters!" he yelled, jerking his hand away from his sister. "Maybe those are three giant canoes! But how did they ever find such big trees to carve?"

"Is it the Caribs, Father?" asked Atabey.

"No, child," her father said. "These are men we have not seen before." The family watched as the

▲
Taino collar.

people on the three wooden ships got into smaller boats and started paddling to shore.

"Mother, look at how white their skin is!" Atabey cried. "And what is that strange hair growing out of their chins?"

"Why do they hide their bodies behind that colored cloth?" asked Bagua. "Do they have feet?"

One of the strangers, a tall man with gray hair, walked onto the sand. He kneeled and kissed the ground. The other strangers followed him. "Is that their chief, Father?" Atabey asked. "Mother, what are those long poles with the colored sheets on top that they're sticking into the sand?"

Atabey's parents had no answers. Some of the children from the village ran up to the strangers and pinched their pale skin to see if they were real. The strangers spoke, but no one understood their words.

The strangers gave gifts to Atabey's people that they had never seen before—red caps, glass beads, and little brass bells. Atabey learned that the tall man was indeed their chief. The strangers seemed very interested in the gold objects her people wore. Atabey was confused. Everyone in the village seemed to welcome the strangers. But were these the people of the chief's vision? Would these people cause them harm?

QUESTIONS TO CONSIDER

1. How did the Taino prepare for celebrations?

2. How did the Taino pass down their history from one generation to the next? How does that affect what we know about them?

3. What were the "monsters with white wings" that the Taino saw approaching their island?

4. Why do you think Atabey was so worried about the visitors? Was she right to worry? Explain.

Columbus on the Taino

When he returned from his first voyage to the Americas in 1492, Christopher Columbus described in a letter the people he had met.

They are simple and generous with what they have, to such a degree as no one would believe but him who had seen it. Of anything they have, if it be asked for, they never say no, but do rather invite the person to accept it, and show as much lovingness as though they would give their hearts. And whether it be a thing of value, or one of little worth, they are straightways content with whatsoever trifle of whatsoever kind may be given them in return for it. I forbade that anything so worthless as fragments of broken platters, and pieces of broken glass, and strap buckles, should be given them; although when they were able to get such things, they seemed to think they had the best jewel in the world.

The Peacemaker
and the People of
the Longhouse

BY MARY KATHLEEN FLYNN

The Peacemaker watched sadly as the young men came home from war. When the women and children of the village came out to greet the returning warriors, he heard the wailing cries of those whose fathers, brothers, husbands, and sons had been killed. This made the Peacemaker very sad.

That night the nation held a council. The younger people all wanted to go out to war again the next day. The Peacemaker begged them to stop fighting. He had traveled a long way from his own country in the north to bring a message of peace to the warring nations.

People and Terms to Know

Peacemaker—messenger sometimes known as Deganawidah (day•gah•nah•WEE•duh). He helped bring together the warring Onondaga, Mohawk, Cayuga, Oneida, and Seneca nations in a league. (See the note on page 174.)

This wampum belt, sometimes called the "Hiawatha belt," commemorates
the founding of the League of the Haudenosaunee, the People of the
Longhouse. At the center is the Tree of the Great Peace, linking the nations

The Peacemaker tried to explain his message, but when he spoke, his ideas flew much faster than his words. He struggled to find words to express his thoughts, but the words would not come. The people did not listen to him.

He knew that he needed strength today because he had another long journey ahead of him.

The next morning, the Peacemaker woke up before dawn. He made a fire and cooked a big breakfast of corn, squash, and beans. He knew that he needed strength today because he had another long journey ahead of him. If this nation would not listen to his message of peace, perhaps another nation would. When the sun rose, he left and headed west.

The Peacemaker walked all day over gently rolling hills and through thick forests. At sunset, he came to a lake. He knelt at the edge of the lake and scooped up water in his hands and drank it. He drank for a long time. He ate some wild blackberries that he found growing near the shore. Then he lay down to rest. Everything was quiet and peaceful.

The Peacemaker was awakened by the sound of a canoe paddle dipping in the water. He sat up and looked out across the lake. A man was approaching in a canoe. The man looked like he was from the **Onondaga** nation.

The man paddled his canoe to shore and removed a basket filled with white and purple shell beads. He began to string the beads together in different patterns. The Peacemaker watched him a long time, wondering what the man was doing with the beads.

Finally, the Peacemaker gave in to his curiosity. He stood up and walked over to the man. The Peacemaker told the man his name and that he had come from far away with a message of peace for the warring nations. The man said his name was **Hiawatha**, and that he was from the Onondaga nation.

Hiawatha told the Peacemaker that the string of shell beads was **wampum**. He strung wampum, he explained, to help people who were mourning their dead to remember certain comforting words.

People and Terms to Know

Onondaga (AHN•uhn•DAW•guh)—Native American nation of central New York State.

Hiawatha (hy•uh•WAH•thuh)—Onondaga who became a leader of the Mohawk nation and helped the Peacemaker spread his ideas among the warring nations.

wampum—strings of shell beads. Wampum was later used by Native American peoples in belts to record important events.

The Peacemaker saw that Hiawatha shared his wish for peace. The two new friends made a plan. The Peacemaker had many ideas about how to unite the warring nations, and Hiawatha was a good speaker who could capture people's attention. They decided to travel together. They would bring their message of peace to the five nations that were always at war: the Mohawk, Cayuga, Oneida, Onondaga, and Seneca.

They would bring their message of peace to the five nations that were always at war.

First, they went to the **Mohawk** nation and asked to speak to the council. Hiawatha first spoke to council about peace, but the Mohawk were not convinced.

Then the Peacemaker asked one of the warriors for an arrow. Holding it above his head so that all the people could see, the Peacemaker broke it in half easily. Next, he took five arrows and bound them together. He asked a warrior to break the arrows, but the bundle was too strong to break. Other warriors also tried and failed to break the bundle of arrows. The Peacemaker told the

People and Terms to Know

Mohawk—Native American nation that was the first to accept the principles of peace and unity brought by the Peacemaker. Their homeland is in what is now central New York State.

Mohawk council that if the five nations would come together, like the bundle of arrows, they would be very strong.

The Mohawks were won over. They were the first of the five nations to agree to live in peace with the others in a league. Then the Peacemaker and Hiawatha went to the **Oneida** nation. They explained that the nations would all live together peacefully, like different families in a **longhouse**. The two friends said that everyone would have to agree before an important decision could be made. They spoke with such strong feeling that they won over the Oneida.

Then the Oneida leader went with the Peacemaker and Hiawatha to the next nation, the **Cayuga**. The Cayuga had also lost many warriors in battle and they welcomed the idea of peace. The Cayuga agreed to join the league.

Next, the two friends went to the Seneca nation. They, too, wanted to join the league.

People and Terms to Know

Oneida (oh•NY•duh)—Native American nation of central New York State.

longhouse—long building usually built of poles and bark and housing several families. It was used especially by the nations of the Haudenosaunee, or Iroquois.

Cayuga (ky•YOO•guh)—Native American nation of central New York State.

▲ Iroquois people build a new longhouse next to another one in this reconstruction.

Finally, the Peacemaker and Hiawatha went to the Onondaga. They had saved this nation for last because they knew that the Onondaga leader, named **Tadadaho**, was very powerful. He was also said to be so evil that his body was twisted and snakes grew from his head.

When they first told Tadadaho about the league of nations, the news made him very angry. He did not want to give up any of his power.

But the Peacemaker and Hiawatha talked to Tadadaho for a long time. They showed him the five

People and Terms to Know

Tadadaho (TAH•dah•DAH•hoh)—leader of the Onandaga. His name became the title of the leader of the League.

arrows bound together, and they explained that the nations would live together as if they were families sharing a longhouse. Still Tadadaho refused.

Finally, the Peacemaker and Hiawatha promised to give the Onondaga more representatives in the council of the league than any of the other nations. The Onondaga would become Keepers of the Council Fire and keep the wampum belts that contained the laws of the league and the records of the council's meetings. That made Tadadaho feel much better, and he agreed.

* * *

The Mohawk, the Oneida, the Cayuga, the Seneca, and the Onondaga became the Five Nations of the **Haudenosaunee**, "People of the Long House." The People of the Long House lived together peacefully for hundreds of years.

People and Terms to Know

Haudenosaunee (how•dehn•oh•SAW•nee)—literally, "People Building a Longhouse," league of five Native American nations often referred to as the Iroquois League. A sixth nation, the Tuscarora, later joined the league.

1. In what way was Hiawatha's wampum important to the founding of the league of the Five Nations?

2. How did the Peacemaker and Hiawatha use the longhouse and the bundle of arrows to explain the league?

3. How did the two friends persuade Tadadaho to join the league?

4. Why do you think the Five Nations agreed to the peace pact?

▲ Two Iroquois warriors approach the Onondaga chief Tadadaho. In this early drawing, he is pictured as a sorceror with snakes for hair.

The Council of the Great Peace

Native American oral tradition preserves the words with which the Peacemaker opened the Council of the Great Peace, which established the League of the Haudenosaunee.

I am Deganawidah and with the Five Nations' Confederate Lords I plant the Tree of Great Peace. . . . I name the tree the Tree of the Great Long Leaves. . . . Roots have spread out from the Tree of the Great Peace, one to the north, one to the east, one to the south and one to the west. The name of these roots is The Great White Roots and their nature is Peace and Strength.

If any man or any nation outside the Five Nations shall obey the laws of the Great Peace and make known their disposition to the Lords of the Confederacy, they may trace the Roots to the Tree and if their minds are clean and they are obedient and promise to obey the wishes of the Confederate Council, they shall be welcomed to take shelter beneath the Tree of the Long Leaves.

The Adventures of Estevanico

BY WALTER HAZEN

The date was March 7, 1539. The place was New Galicia, in western Mexico, a part of New Spain in America. Two men were preparing to set out on a great adventure. One was a **Franciscan** priest. The other was a black man from Morocco, in North Africa. The priest wore a robe of gray cloth. The black man was dressed in bright colors and had jingle bells attached to his wrists and ankles. With him, in the manner of a lord out hunting, were two greyhounds.

Who were these two men, and upon what great adventure were they about to set out? The priest was Friar Marcos de Niza, who had searched for

---

People and Terms to Know

Franciscan—member of a religious order founded by St. Francis of Assisi in 1209.

Born in North Africa, Estevanico explored parts of North America with the Spanish.

gold earlier in the New World. The black man was **Estevanico**, or "Little Steven." The purpose of their adventure? To locate the Seven Cities of Cibola, seven Indian cities in what is now New Mexico, that were said to be full of treasure.

Misfortune struck Narváez's group from the start.

Estevanico was born about 1503 in the Moroccan town of Azamor. In 1513, he was captured by Spanish soldiers and brought to Spain, where he became the personal servant of a nobleman named Andres Dorantes. The two became close friends. In 1528, Dorantes and his servant accompanied the explorer Panfilo de Narváez on an expedition to America. Narváez had received five ships from the King of Spain with orders to explore and settle Florida. Estevanico and Andres Dorantes were aboard one of these ships when it arrived near what is now Tampa Bay, in April 1528.

Misfortune struck Narváez's group from the start. They came under constant attack from Indians. They also had to cope with heat, insects,

---

People and Terms to Know

Estevanico (EHST•ah•van•EE•koh)—(c. 1503–1539) African slave who became a guide and interpreter for the Spanish in the New World.

and deep swamps. They finally fought their way to where Tallahassee is today, losing almost half their number along the way. When they were cut off from their ships, they marched south to the Gulf of Mexico. There they built five crude rafts and set sail west along the coast.

Once again disaster struck the group. They were caught in a storm off the coast of present-day Texas, and the rafts sank. Narváez and all except four men drowned. One of the survivors was Estevanico. Another was Andres Dorantes, his master. It is here that the story of Estevanico's adventures in the New World really begins.

Estevanico and his three companions reached an island near what is now Galveston, Texas. They called it "La Isla de Mal Hado," or "Bad Luck Island." After a year on the island, they made their way to the mainland. Once again, they met Indians, who at first were friendly. In time, however, the Indians made slaves of them and used them as bearers to carry heavy loads.

Five years passed before Estevanico and the others were able to escape. During their time of slavery, they lived like their captors. They ate berries, walnuts, prickly pears, and fish. They went around almost naked, and the Indians said they "shed their skins" twice a year like "snakes." (Probably because their skin peeled from constant sunburn.)

After escaping from the Indians in Texas, Estevanico and his friends began the long journey to Mexico. They walked more than 3,000 miles through swamps and deserts to get there. They finally arrived in Mexico City in June 1536.

A large number of Indians went with Estevanico's group to Mexico. These Indians were friendly. They believed Estevanico and his fellow travelers were faith healers who could cure diseases. On many occasions, and to their own surprise, they somehow managed to do just that.

Shortly after arriving in Mexico City, Dorantes sold Estevanico to Antonio de Mendoza, the viceroy (governor) of New Spain. Estevanico had learned many of the Indian languages during his years in the New World, and Mendoza thought he would be a good translator, guide, and scout. He chose Estevanico to go with Friar Marcos in his search for the Seven Cities of Cibola.

In March 1539, the two men set out. They crossed into what is now Arizona and turned east into New Mexico. Their progress was slow. Estevanico grew impatient and asked Marcos if he could go ahead with a small scouting party. The

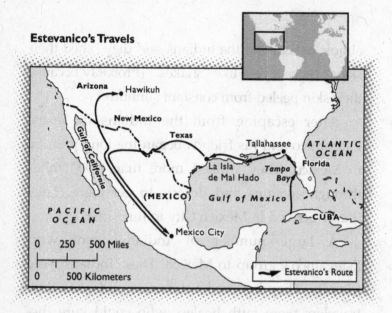

Estevanico's Travels

Arizona · Hawikuh

New Mexico

Texas

Tallahassee

ATLANTIC OCEAN

La Isla de Mal Hado · Tampa Bay · Florida

Gulf of California

(MEXICO) · Gulf of Mexico

PACIFIC OCEAN

CUBA

Mexico City

0   250   500 Miles

0   500 Kilometers

→ Estevanico's Route

friar agreed, and the two explorers made a plan. If Estevanico came upon any good news about finding the seven golden cities, he was to send a large cross to Friar Marcos. If an Indian bearer arrived with a small cross, this meant that Estevanico was no closer to his goal than before.

It meant nothing to Estevanico that he was leading the first European expedition into the great American Southwest. And he probably never thought of the fact that he was the first black man to venture into these parts. All that mattered to Estevanico was gold and the life of leisure it could bring him.

As Estevanico and his scouting party moved deeper into New Mexico, they continued to hear stories of the seven Indian cities. Based on such "facts," Estevanico sent a large cross to Friar Marcos. But Estevanico's information proved false. The Seven Cities of Cibola did not exist. What Estevanico—and later others—saw were really **Zuni** villages that glowed in the sun and only looked like they were made of gold.

Estevanico did not survive the search for the seven cities. He was killed by the Indians in the Zuni village of Hawikuh. He may have been killed because the medicine rattle he carried was trimmed with owl feathers, which the Zuni considered to be a sign of death, or evil. Whatever the reason, the black man who opened up the American Southwest did not live to understand how important his expedition was for the explorers who followed him.

QUESTIONS TO CONSIDER

1. Where were the Seven Cities of Cibola thought to be? Why were explorers looking for them?

2. How was Estevanico brought to the New World? Why?

3. What did the Seven Cities of Cibola turn out to be?

People and Terms to Know

Zuni—tribe of American Indians in what is now western New Mexico.

Sources

A Search for Early Americans *by Judith Conaway*

The dig in this story is fictional—it doesn't even have a name. The characters are fictional, too, but all of the science is real. The story tells about the latest discoveries in archaeology today. Good sources of additional information include: *The Settlement of the Americas: A New Prehistory* by Thomas D. Dillehay (New York: Basic Books, 2000); *Boats, Bones, and Bison: Archaeology and the First Colonization of Western North America* by E. James Dixon (University of New Mexico Press, 2000); and *Ancient North America: The Archaeology of a Continent* by Brian M. Fagan (Thomas & Hudson, 2000).

Clovis Hunters Kill a Mammoth *by Walter Hazen*

All the characters in the story are fictional. The mammoth hunt, however, is depicted as it might have occurred. Good sources of further information include Peter Farb's *Man's Rise to Civilization as Shown by the Indians of North America from Primeval Times to the Coming of the Industrial State* (New York: E.P. Dutton & Co., Inc., 1968) and David Hurst Thomas's *Exploring Native North America* (New York: Oxford University Press, 2000).

Carvers of the Mound Builders *by Barbara Littman*

All the characters in the story are fictional. The picture of Hopewell Indian life is based on archeological evidence. For more information, see *Americans Before Columbus* by Elizabeth Chesley Baity (New York: 1961); *Mound Builders of Ancient America: The Archaeology of a Myth* by Robert Silverberg (Greenwich, CT: New York Graphic Society, 1968); and *The Mound Builders* by William E. Scheele (New York: World Publishing Co., 1960).

The Wrong Sister: A Tale of the Mound Builders
by Fitzgerald Higgins

All the characters in the story are fictional. The picture of life in Cahokia is based on archeological evidence. For more information, see *Cahokia: City of the Sun* by Claudia G. Mink (Cahokia Mounds Museum Society, 1992); *Cahokia: The Great American Metropolis* by Bilone Whiting Young and Melvin L. Fowler (Champaign-Urbana: University of Illinois Press, 1999); and *Native Americans Before 1492: The Mound Building Centers of the Eastern Woodlands* by Lynda Norene Shaffer and Kevin Reilly (M.E. Sharpe, 1992).

The Anasazi Prepare for Company *by Judith Lloyd Yero*

Johnny is a fictional character. The description of Anasazi life and the gathering at Chaco Canyon is historically accurate. An excellent source of information on the Anasazi is W. M. Ferguson and A. H. Rohn's *Anasazi Ruins of the Southwest in Color* (Albuquerque, NM: University of New Mexico Press, 1987).

The Hero Twins of the Mayan Sacred Ball Game
by Dee Masters

All of the characters in this story are fictional, but their ball game and its importance in Mayan society are real. A wonderful source of information on the Mayan culture is Ralph Nelson's translation of *The Popol Vuh: the Great Mythological Book of the Ancient Maya* (Boston: Houghton Mifflin, 1976).

The Legend of Quetzalcoatl *by Mary Kathleen Flynn*

The narrator and her parents are fictional characters, but the city and palace they live in are real. This version of the life and legend of the priest-ruler Quetzalcoatl, who led the Toltecs during the tenth century, is based *on The Course of Mexican History, Sixth Edition,* by Michael C. Meyer, William L. Sherman, and Susan M. Deeds (New York and Oxford: Oxford University Press, 1999).

The Emperor and the Hummingbird *by Stephen Currie*

The narrator and his friend are fictional, but the description of Aztec life in Tenochtitlán is accurate. A good source of information about this time is *The Daily Life of the Aztecs On the Eve of The Spanish Conquest* by Jacques Soustelle (New York: MacMillan, 1962). Also see the sources listed for "The Story of Malinche" for more information on the Aztecs and their rise and fall.

Pachacuti, Inca Empire Builder *by Walter Hazen*

The narrator of the story is fictitious. Virocha Inca and Inca Yupanqui are historical figures. More information on this time and place can be found in Loren McIntyre's *The Incredible Incas and Their Timeless Land* (Washington, D.C.: National Geographic Society, 1975), Matthew W. Stirling's *Indians of the Americas* (Washington, D.C.: National Geographic Society, 1955), and Jonathan Norton Leonard's *Ancient America* (New York: Time Incorporated, 1967).

The Story of Malinche *by Jane Leder*

Malinche was a real historical figure, and while elements of her story are still questioned to this day, there are many sources of information about her life and her role in the conquest of Mexico. Among them are Cortés' *Five Letters of Cortes to the Emperor Charles V* (W. W. Norton, 1969) and Ben Hulses' "End of an Empire: The Spanish Conquest of Mexico," in *The Concord Review.*

New Life in Vinland *by Brian J. Mahoney*

This story is a fictional account based on events and characters in the Norse sagas, or tales, written in Iceland. Scientists have found Viking ruins and artifacts on the northern coast of North America, in Newfoundland. Many of the descriptions of Vinland in the Norse sagas seem to fit this area. The Viking settlement in Vinland did not last very long. Greatly outnumbered by the Native Americans, who did not want the settlers to stay, the Vikings returned to Greenland. For more information on the Vikings, see *From Viking to Crusader, The Scandinavians and Europe 800–1200* (New York, NY: Rizzoli, 1992).

Hopi Migrations *by Stephen Currie*

The characters and events in this story come from the oral tradition of the Hopi people. For further information, see *Book of the Hopi* by Frank Waters (New York: Viking Press, 1985); and *The Fourth World of the Hopis: The Epic Story of the Hopi Indians as Preserved in Legends and Traditions* by Harold Courlander (University of New Mexico Press, 1987).

The Taino See Three Ships *by Danny Miller*

Atabey and her family are fictional characters based on accounts of the Taino people at the time of Columbus. This story takes place on October 11 and 12, 1492. The "winged monsters" are the ships of the first voyage of Christopher Columbus, the *Niña*, the *Pinta*, and the *Santa Maria*. For more information, see *The Tainos: Rise and Decline of the People Who Greeted Columbus* by Irving Rouse (New Haven, CT: Yale University Press, 1992) and *The Tainos: The People Who Welcomed Columbus* by Francine Jacobs (New York: G. P. Putnam's Sons, 1992). *The Log of Christopher Columbus* translated by Robert H. Fuson (Camden, Maine: International Marine Publishing, 1992) relates Columbus's reactions to these native people.

The Peacemaker and the People of the Longhouse
by Mary Kathleen Flynn

The Iroquois League was real. The roles that Deganawidah and Hiawatha played in bringing about the League of the Haudenosaunee, or the Iroquois League, are based on legend. The story told here was based on two sources, *The Oxford Companion to United States History*, edited by Paul S. Boyer (Oxford and New York: Oxford University Press, 2001) and *The Great Law and the Longhouse: A Political History of the Iroquois Confederacy* by William Nelson Fenton (University of Oklahoma Press, 1998). Another good source is *Wampum Belts of the Iroquois* by Ray Fadden Tehanetorens (Book Publishing Company, 1999).

The Adventures of Estevanico *by Walter Hazen*

All characters mentioned in the story of Estevanico are historical figures. You can find more information in *Colonial Spanish America: A Documentary History*, edited by Kenneth Mills and William B. Taylor (Wilmington, Delaware: Scholarly Resources, Inc., 1998), Paul Horgan's *Conquistadors in North American History* (New York: Farrar, Straus and Company, 1963), and *African Americans in Florida* by Maxine D. Jones and Kevin M. McCarthy (Sarasota, Florida: Pineapple Press, Inc., 1993).

Glossary of People and Terms to Know

Acoma Pueblo (AH•kuh•muh PWEH•bloh)—village on top of a mesa (flat-topped mountain) in what is now New Mexico. The Acoma are known for their beautiful white pottery decorated in black. Pueblo refers to an Indian community characterized by buildings of adobe. Pueblos are found in the southwestern United States.

Anasazi (ah•nah•SAH•zee)—Navajo word meaning "ancient people" or "ancient enemies." The Anasazi were a group of Native Americans who settled in the southwestern region of the United States. Their culture went through several stages beginning about A.D. 100.

ancestors (AN•sehs•tuhrz)—people from whom one is descended; early members of one's family; forerunners.

aqueducts—large stone structures through which water flows from mountainous areas into cities.

archaeology (AHR•kee•AHL•uh•jee)—study of ancient civilizations. Scientists who study archaeology are known as archaeologists.

areytos (AHR•ee•YEHT•ohz)—Taino celebration involving songs and dances.

artifacts—human-made objects remaining from early civilizations. Even broken pieces of artifacts interest archaeologists.

atlatl (aht•LAHT•l)—spear-throwing device usually made of a stick with a thong or socket to hold the spear steady. It added force to the spear-thrower's thrust.

bison (BY•suhn)—large hoofed mammal having a dark brown coat, shaggy mane, and short, curved horns; also known as buffalo.

burial mound—mound of earth in which the dead were buried.

cacao (kuh•KOW)—South American tree used in making cocoa and chocolate.

Cahokia (kuh•HOH•kee•uh)—name given by archaeologists to an ancient American Indian city in southwestern Illinois.

calpulli—section of an Aztec city; neighborhood.

canals—manmade waterways used to water fields or for shipping or travel. The original site of Tenochtitlán was an island in the middle of Lake Texcoco. Over the years, Aztecs built many roads and bridges to connect the city to the mainland. Canals dug throughout the city provided good transportation.

carbon dating—method of finding the age of an object by measuring two types of carbon atoms it contains. Because the ratio of these two atoms changes after a living thing dies, scientists can use the measurement to figure out how long ago the living materials in it died.

Caribs—tribal enemies of the Taino.

Casa Rinconada (KAH•sah RIHN•koh•NAH•dah)—large ceremonial kiva in the Chaco Canyon complex in what is now northwestern New Mexico. It was more than 60 feet in diameter and was partly underground. The flat roof was several feet above the ground and was supported by 4 pillars inside the structure.

cassava (kuh•SAH•vah)—tropical plant that was a staple of the Taino diet. Also called manioc.

Cayuga (ky•YOO•guh)—Native American nation of central New York State.

Chaco Canyon (CHAH•koh KAN•yuhn)—now a national park in northwestern New Mexico, Chaco Canyon was once the site of a major Anasazi settlement.

Charles V—(1500–1558) King of Spain. Cortés conquered Mexico in his name.

clans—large groups of families that claim a common ancestor.

Clovis culture—way of life that was followed by ancient people who hunted large animals using spears. The culture is named for Clovis, New Mexico, the first site in the Americas where human weapons were found along with the bones of Ice Age animals.

coiling—way of making rope or twine from plant fibers by twisting multiple strands around each other.

Cortés, Hernán—(c. 1485–1547) Spanish captain who conquered Mexico in the 1500s.

Courts of Creation—in Mayan culture, the universe.

Cuzco—name of both the capital city of the Incas and the valley in which their civilization developed.

dialects—regional variations of a language.

door on the top of your heads—Hopi believed that the earliest human beings were able to communicate with the Creator through soft spots on the tops of their heads.

Erik the Red—(950–1001) Norse chief, explorer, and colonizer.

Estevanico (EHST•ah•van•EE•koh)—(c. 1503–1539) enslaved African who became a guide and interpreter for the Spanish in the New World.

excavation (EX•kuh•VAY•shuhn)—process of digging out or uncovering ancient ruins; an archaeological site or dig.

fertile (FUR•tl)—able to produce crops.

flood plain—flat land that borders a river and is made of soil deposited during floods.

Franciscan—member of a religious order founded by St. Francis of Assisi in 1209.

Greenland—large island off northeast Canada, lying mostly within the Arctic Circle. Greenland was discovered, named, and settled by the Norse chief Erik the Red in about A.D. 986. According to one of the sagas, he called it Greenland because "people would be attracted to go there if it had a favorable name."

Haudenosaunee (how•dehn•oh•SAW•nee)—literally, "People Building a Longhouse," league of five Native American nations often referred to as the Iroquois League. A sixth nation, the Tuscarora, later joined the league.

Hiawatha—(hy•uh•WAH•thuh)—Onondaga who became a leader of the Mohawk nation and helped the Peacemaker spread his ideas among the warring nations.

Ice Age—part of geological time when the earth's temperature was colder, causing large parts of the planet to be covered in glaciers (huge masses of ice). It ended about 10,000 years ago.

Iceland—island in the Atlantic Ocean, 620 miles west of Norway and 185 miles east of Greenland. Iceland was settled by Vikings in the ninth century.

iguanas (ih•GWAH•nuhz)—large tropical lizards.

in situ (ihn SY•too)—Latin for "in place." Archaeologists document their discoveries exactly as they are found. No one can move artifacts until they have been measured and photographed *in situ*. This helps the archaeologists to date the artifacts and to prove the layers have not been disturbed.

jade—gemstone that is usually green or white.

kachinas (kah•CHEE•nahz)—supernatural beings that, according to the Pueblo myths, taught and guided their ancestors. (See page 145.)

kiva (KEE•vah)—Hopi word referring to a circular room that is below ground. Early peoples lived in these pit houses. Later, they were used by family groups for meetings, rituals, storytelling, the instruction of children, and the making of tools and clothing.

Leif—(975–1020) Leif Eriksson, son of Erik the Red. Leif Eriksson discovered a land he called Vinland in the northern part of North America in about 1000.

longhouse—long building where many families lived.

Lords of Death—Mayan gods of the underworld. Each represented a form of death.

Machu Picchu—fortress/city built high in the Andes Mountains of what is now Peru.

maize (mayz)—corn.

Malinche (mah•LIHN•chay)—Aztec slave woman (c. 1500) who became the translator for Spanish conquistador Hernán Cortés.

mammoths—large elephant-like animals that once lived in North America. They became extinct in prehistoric times.

Mayan—of or belonging to the Native American people whose ancient civilization in Central America reached its peak from A.D. 300–900 in Mexico, Belize, Guatemala, and parts of El Salvador and Honduras. Mayan people continue to live in these lands today.

Mendoza, Antonio de—(c. 1490–1552) Viceroy of New Spain from 1535 to 1550 who promoted exploration.

mica (MY•kuh)—shiny rock that can be split into large sheets. The Mound Builders got it from the area of present-day North Carolina.

migrations—movements of groups of people from place to place.

Mohawk—Native American nation that was the first to accept the principles of peace preached by the Peacemaker. Their homeland is in what is now central New York state.

Monte Verde—archaeological site located near the coast of southern Chile where evidence of human life dates back to about 11,700 B.C.

Montezuma—(c. 1480–1520) last ruler of the Aztec Empire.

Mound Builders—group of early North American people who developed a way of life in the Ohio and Mississippi valleys from around 500–400 B.C. to 1500 A.D.

Norway—country in northern Europe occupying the western and northern parts of the Scandinavian peninsula.

obsidian (uhb•SIHD•ee•uhn)— shiny, black glass of volcanic origin.

Oneida (oh•NY•duh)—Native American nation of central New York State.

Onondaga(AHN•uhn•DAW•guh)— Native American nation of central New York State.

Peacemaker—messenger some-times known as Deganawidah (day•gah•nah•WEE•duh). He helped bring together the warring Onondaga, Mohawk, Cayuga, Oneida, and Seneca nations in a league. (See the note on page 174.)

peat—partly decayed form of plant matter that is found in swamps and bogs. Peat provides a wet, oxygen-free environment, protecting materials from bacteria and decay.

petroglyphs—carvings in rock; each clan had its own symbol, such as a coyote for the Coyote Clan.

pipestone—soft, red stone found in Minnesota, the Dakotas, and in Canada. The Mound Builders used it for carving.

pok-a-tok—Mayan ball game that had religious meaning as well as entertainment value.

prairies—wide, level areas of flat or rolling grassland, especially the large plain of central North America.

puma—large wildcat found in many parts of North and South America.

Quetzalcoatl (keht•sa•koh•AT•ihl)—high priest and ruler of the Toltecs, who named himself after the Feathered Serpent god. Legend says that he flashed into the heavens and became the morning star, promising to return one day to rule again.

rampart—wide, raised mound of earth. Ramparts are often built as protection from floods.

saber-toothed tiger—large Ice Age cat with two very long upper teeth.

saplings (SAP•lihngz)—young trees.

shroud—cloth used to wrap a body for burial.

sipapu (SEE•pah•poo)—in Pueblo cultures, a small hole in the floor of a special ceremonial room. The hole represents the place where the Anasazi ancestors came out from inside the earth.

sites—places; archaeological sites are places where scientists dig up objects from ancient human life.

Skraelings—Viking term for Native Americans.

Sotuknang—in Hopi tradition, the nephew of the Creator and the first being created. He organized the universe and directed the creation of the first people, then he gave them speech and wisdom.